OSITION CITY

PANAMA

PACIFIC

EXPOSITION

RANCISCO

PINGREE-TRAUNG CO. LITH. S.F.

THE UNIVERSITY CLUB
OF SAN FRANCISCO

CENTENNIAL HISTORY
1890-1990

THE UNIVERSITY CLUB OF SAN FRANCISCO

CENTENNIAL HISTORY 1890-1990

Mitchell P. Postel

*with an appendix on the clubhouse
by Kevin Tierney*

UNIVERSITY CLUB, SAN FRANCISCO, 1000

Centennial History © University Club, San Francisco 1990
Appendix on the Clubhouse © Kevin Tierney 1990

ISBN 0-962-75400-5

Published by University Club, 800 Powell Street, San Francisco, California 94108, U.S.A.

Designed by Jim Reader
Design and production in association with
Book Production Consultants, 47 Norfolk Street, Cambridge CB1 2LE

Reproduced, printed and bound in Great Britain by
BPCC Hazell Books
Aylesbury, Bucks, England
Member of BPCC Ltd.

ENDPAPERS: *In this magnificent map, drawn in 1912 for the Panama Pacific
International Exposition, the University Club is shown almost dead center,
directly below the Fairmont Hotel.*

Table of Contents

Preface vii

Introduction ix

1 Beginnings 1
Uncle Billy's Idea 1
The Name 3
Getting Down to Business 3
The Urge to Belong 5
First Meetings, First Clubhouse 5
A Peek Inside 6
Notes 8

2 Paying for Pleasure 11
Finances and Board Responsibilities 11
Recruiting New Members 13
Locomotive Smith 13
The Fate of the Ladies 14
The Pre-1906 Search for a New Home 14
Notes 16

3 Earthquake and Relocation 19
Temporary Quarters 19
House Hunting 21
A New Home in a Stable 22
Building 800 Powell 23

Grand Opening 24
Early Years at 800 Powell 25
Until the War 26
Hermes Joins the Club 27
Notes 28

4 Prewar, War, Postwar 31
A Faraway Fight 31
Entering the Fray 31
The Beginning of the Drought 32
Armistice and Peace: Normalcy 33
Notes 33

5 Prohibition 35
The Lockers 36
The Clubhouse Interior 36
A Fine Gift 37
Mr Interlocutor, Sah! 38
The Excesses of 1927 39
The Business of the "Roaring" Twenties 40
Notes 43

6 Depression 45
The One-and-a-Halfs and the Repeal of
    Prohibition 45
A New Generation Takes Over 46

Some Depressing Aspects of the
  Depression 47
A Little Light at the End of the Tunnel 48
The Shambles 49
The Ladies' Annex That Never Was 49
Notes 51

7 War Again 53
An Overgenerous Club 53
A Fantastic Redeployment of Nob Hill 53
An Uncomfortable Presidency 54
De Fremery and the Crisis 55
The Club's Shabbiest Hour 57
The Free Dinner 57
Notes 58

8 Peace and Prosperity 59
Renaissance 59
Riding High 60
Debt Reduction and an Acquisition 61
The Developers Cometh 64
In the Black 65
Sending in a Marine 65
Notes 66

9 The Sixties 67
Inflation Erodes the Club's Position 67
Master of its own House 67
Schaefer's Folly 68
From Schaefer's Folly to Hermes' Garden ... 68
In Vino Felicitas 69
The 830 Powell Street Controversy,
  Part One 69
Notes 71

10 The Contentious Seventies 73
The 830 Powell Street Controversy,
  Part Two 73

Back to Ordinary Business 75
Labor Costs and the Club Institute 75
New Squash Courts 76
Hermes Lost and Found 77
Notes 78

11 Modern Times 79
The Battle of the Sexes 79
The Continuing Life of the Club 83
Notes 86

12 Club Life 89
The Staff 89
The Members 91
Notes 92

A Note on Sources 93
University Club Publications 93
Archival and Documentary Sources 93
Informal Sources 94
General San Francisco and
  California Sources 94
Comparative Sources 94
Picture Sources 94

The Clubhouse by Kevin Tierney 97
The Architects 97
The Site 97
The Exterior 99
The Interior 99
Selected Surviving Original Features of the
  Clubhouse Interior 99
Principal Interior Changes to the Clubhouse
  since 1909 100
An Appraisal 101
Notes 101

Preface

When the Board of Directors asked me to oversee the publication of this *Centennial History*, I accepted on condition that an outsider would be commissioned to write it. My concern was with the credibility of the work. Although excellent histories of some other clubs have been written by their own members, two considerations favored an independent author. First, it seemed to me that a non-member would be less vulnerable to any accusation of bias. Secondly, hiring a professional writer would emphasize the importance of the Club's history. Any institution which survives a century is worthy of note - and in spite of some close calls, the University Club of San Francisco *has* survived.

Mr Mitchell P. Postel, the Executive Director of the San Mateo County Historical Association, an experienced local historian, agreed to research the Club's story and commit it to paper, and the result vindicates the judgment that he was the right man for the job. Not being a member of the Club, Mr Postel wrestled gamely with the somewhat confusing vocabulary which it has developed over the years. Now, he knows as well as any member that the drink called a "one-and-a-half" goes by the same name as a regular Club event; that the Economic Round Table must be distinguished from the "round table" at the fourth-floor bar and that Boxing Night and Boxing Day are as different as, well, night and day.

Of course, his account reflects surviving records,

notwithstanding that anecdote, folklore and private information might put a different light on some events. Documents and other records (including oral histories) are often incomplete and unrepresentative, but they are the raw material from which history is created and the rest tends to fall by the wayside; for many important unrecorded aspects of Club life, readers must depend on their own recollections. The innumerable "clubs within the Club", overlapping and ever-changing, formed by members over the years endure only as memories in the minds of the participants.

As things turned out, Mr Postel encountered quite unforeseen difficulties in gaining access to some archives. As this history was being prepared, the earthquake of 1989 occurred, not quite as envisaged by Curt Gentry's *The Last Days of the Late Great State of California* (1968), but disconcerting nonetheless. In consequence, the main branch of the San Francisco Public Library was closed for over four months (until the end of February 1990), preventing access to the History Room's collection of local materials, including its pictures. And at the same time the California Historical Society's internal politics put it in such turmoil that none of its resources has been available.

Despite these hindrances, Mr Postel managed to do extensive research, as this book attests. The tale he tells shows that although the Club has had many ups and downs, continuity predominates: *plus ca change, plus c'est la meme chose*. Recurrent themes echo down the years: the Club's bar is more lucrative than its dining-room; official occasions vacillate between huge successes and total flops; some members use the Club seldom and dislike paying their bills and a few use it a lot without paying their bills. Cost estimates for Club projects nearly always turn out to be too low; rarely can the Club's finances truly be described as sound. The fact that the Club has successfully dealt with these constants during its first century augurs well for its second.

Kevin Tierney

Introduction

The first history of San Francisco's University Club was written by member Nathaniel Blaisdell in 1932, and updated by the addition of a chapter entitled "Through New Deal and War to the Atomic Age" by member Lewis P. Mansfield in 1954. Blaisdell explained about his work:

> The facts here are set down from memory and by comparison and are obtained in part from those of the founders and charter members who are still living. No attempt is made to follow the historic tradition. The aim of the compiler is to discover and detail the facts and fancies, stories and gossip of the Club....

Thus, his short history, valuable as it is, did not purport to be systematically researched or comprehensive. It was, rather, anecdotal and informal and he modestly left "to the future historian the task of rearranging, rejecting, reconciling and realizing a worthy history".

This *Centennial History* tries to outline the Club's story using existing primary sources and putting it into the wider context of American, Californian and San Franciscan social history.

At certain points, controversies within the Club have been tumultuous: but through it all, members have stuck together in an environment of *camaraderie* that is quite exemplary. The present writer, who has completed several organization histories (the Burlingame Country Club, 1982; the San Francisco Rotary Club, 1983; the San Mateo County Historical Association, 1985; and the San Mateo County Community College District, 1987), has never encountered debates of quite such passion as those at the University Club. Certainly, some of these instances of internal discord would have toppled a weaker institution: yet, perhaps because of the Club's original purpose in bringing educated minds together, it has tolerated differences of opinion among members without the fear that it would fall apart. All members, whatever side they have taken on particular issues, share a deep pride in the Club. As it heads into its second century, the Club remains as vital as ever and the present writer is deeply grateful for the opportunity that he has had to interpret its first hundred years.

Mitchell P. Postel

CHAPTER 1

Beginnings

S everal notable things happened in San Francisco in 1890: the city's first "skyscraper" was topped off at the corner of Market and Kearny Streets;[1] construction of a seawall at the foot of Powell Street began; the police department installed its first traffic signal boxes; and King Kalakaua of Hawaii paid a visit. But for the purposes of this narrative, by far the most momentous event was the founding of the University Club.

Uncle Billy's Idea

The Club had its beginnings at a dinner held by the Harvard Club of San Francisco on Thursday, July 17, 1890 at the *Maison Doree* restaurant on Kearny Street.[2] There, explained Nathaniel Blaisdell, the Club's first historian, the chef's daughter, Helen Dingeon — "the spritely prima donna of the 'Old Tivoli' and the successor of Lotta as San Francisco's sweetheart" — was as much of an attraction as the celebrated cuisine.

But foundation of the University Club was not a project of the Harvard Club. I.F. Barreda Sherman, whose father was an early member of the University Club, credited the idea of its formation to one man, William Thomas (Harvard, class of 1873).[3] Although the University Club's motto came to be *multarum filii matrum*, Thomas's almost singlehanded initiative in bringing the Club into existence makes him the

"Uncle Billy" Thomas (1853-1936), the University Club's founder and first President. Unlike many clubs, the University Club does not have a "rogues' gallery" of past Presidents; this picture was unearthed from San Francisco: Its Builders Past and Present *(1913).*

The Club's birth certificate, August 8, 1890.

Club's "father" and would justify another motto. However, since Thomas is known affectionately within the Club as "uncle Billy", not "father William", the Club's motto remains unchanged.

Thomas's experience as president of the San Francisco Harvard Club for a number of years led him to believe that the time had come to form a club where all college men could get together. And so *alumni* of other institutions were invited to the Harvard Club's midsummer dinner, most conspicuously several from the naval academy at Annapolis and its military counterpart at West Point.

Shortly before midnight,[4] Thomas made his pitch. He had prepared his ground well; according to Blaisdell, his proposition was accepted "with enthusiasm". Those present elected Thomas as President and Harold Wheeler (Harvard, class of 1877) as Secretary.[5] Two days later, the men held an organizational meeting at the law offices of Chickering & Gregory in the First National Bank building at the corner of Bush and Sansome Streets. On August 8, California's Secretary of State William C. Hendricks signed the necessary articles of incorporation and the University Club of San Francisco became a legal entity.

The Name

Why that name? In part, it reflected the huge expansion of opportunities for higher education that followed the Civil War: and the name connoted an identifiable affinity group.[6] San Francisco's University Club was founded in the great age of Club formation; nearly every American city has at least one club founded between 1865 and 1900 which is called "University Club" or might just as well be.[7] The name was chosen, not just in San Francisco but across the nation, to distinguish such clubs from existing commercial clubs, which were already a feature of every major city by the end of the nineteenth century.[8]

Although San Francisco was not the only city to form a "University Club", it was in no sense a branch of any club elsewhere. Clubs of this name varied widely in their size, tastes and accommodations and continue to do so to this day. For a time the affinity of the country's various University Clubs was ignored, if not unrecognized: but it came to be of significance after the turn of the century when it led to informal contacts among them which benefited members of them all.[9]

Getting Down to Business

Soon after incorporation, other Club officers were appointed. Sidney V. Smith (Yale, class of 1865) was elected First Vice-President. Residing in San Rafael, he was — like Thomas and Wheeler — a San Francisco attorney. Frank Soule (U.S.M.A., class of 1866), was elected Second Vice-President. Francis Carolan (Cornell, class of 1882) was the Club's first Treasurer.[10]

Also on the original board of directors was George F. Harrison (U.S.M.A., class of 1873), then residing at 2507 Sacramento Street and a lieutenant in the United States army. His other colleagues on the Board were three attorneys: Elliott McAllister (California, class of 1884) of the firm of McAllister & McAllister at 328 Montgomery, M. Francis

Michael (Harvard, class of 1887) with an office at 402 Montgomery and Charles J. Swift of the firm of Henley, Swift & Rigby at 101 Sansome.

Apart from its officers, the other charter members of the Club were:

Pelham Ames — an attorney and the secretary of the Sutro Tunnel Company, whose offices were at 320 Sansome Street and who, like First Vice-President Sidney V. Smith, resided in San Rafael.

John Chetwood — an attorney who worked at 318 Pine Street and originally lived in Oakland, but became one of the Club's first permanent boarders after it found quarters.

William H. Chickering (Amherst, class of 1880) — an attorney with the firm of Chickering & Gregory.

Donald Y. Campbell (Yale, class of 1880) — an attorney in the firm of Hutchinson & Campbell at 130 Sansome Street: Campbell lived in Oakland.

James W. Carlin — who lived at 226 Stockton Street and was a retired naval officer.[11]

Albert N. Drown (Brown, class of 1861) — an attorney who practised at 621 Clay Street and lived at 2550 Jackson.

Clinton Day (California, class of 1868) — an architect best remembered for his design of Stanford's Memorial Chapel and the City of Paris department store in San Francisco.

Charles P. Eells — an attorney, who in later life served on the San Francisco Board of Education.[12]

W.W. Foote (Virginia, class of 1865) — an attorney who served as commissioner from California at the Paris Exposition of 1890.

Dirwell Hewitt (Williams, class of 1886) — a special agent for the Orient Insurance Company with an office at 932 Bush Street.

George D. Metcalf — secretary of the Del Monte Milling Company with an office at 107 California Street. Metcalf lived in Oakland.

Hall McAllister (Harvard, class of 1886) — an attorney who shared law offices with his

The first clubhouse at 722 Sutter Street. Nathaniel Blaisdell, the Club's first historian, described it as "a rather stolid mid-Victorian building". At the time the Club leased it, it was owned by William T. Coleman, organizer of San Francisco's Committee of Vigilance in 1856 and 1877.

brother Elliott, a member of the Club's original board.[13]

Henry H. Sherwood (Harvard, class of 1882) — manager of Sherwood and Sherwood of 212-214 Market Street, commission agents specializing in the importation of beverages.[14]

William R. Smedberg — soldier and businessman.[15]

Frank Symmes (Harvard, class of 1867) — businessman.[16]

Some generalizations can be made about the Club's original 24 members. First, most had attended east coast schools, with Harvard predominating: although it subsequently forged close links with local universities, the Club was at its inception a largely Ivy League concoction. Second, the commonest occupation among them was the practice of law: 14 out of the 24 were attorneys. Of the remaining 10, 6 managed some type of business, 3 were in the armed services or had recently retired from them, and 1 was an architect.

The Urge to Belong

Modern readers may ask why the impulse to form associations was so strong. After all, then — as now — San Francisco had enough restaurants and hotel dining rooms to ensure that a man could get a good meal. Yet, such places were not the chosen venue of a gentleman unless a private room was available: in the absence of other distractions, the highlight of most organized nights was an after-dinner speech; this was the great age of after-dinner speaking.[17]

But the greatest impetus to Club formation was the demand for residential facilities which dictated club architecture and underlay the financial viability of most clubs. The conventional living expectations and needs of a man-about-town were different from today's. Well-bred young men did not set up an independent household unless and until they got married: in the meantime, a men's club was the most congenial choice as a place to stay. A house needed servants to run and there were few apartment buildings until the twentieth century. Besides, the men needed only sleeping rooms, not kitchens; few

The interior of 722 Sutter Street. I.F. Barreda Sherman, taken there as a child, remembered the dining room as dark green and that a baron of beef was wheeled round on a cart.

of them had the inclination or skill to cook for themselves, having been brought up in an environment of domestic servants.[18]

First Meetings, First Clubhouse

The Club began meeting on the second floor of a building on Pine Street which had just been vacated by the Bohemian Club. Nathaniel Blaisdell recorded that these premises were unfurnished except for "enough chairs to accommodate the occasional gatherings called to report progress and approve action".

The first order of business was to find a clubhouse, for which purpose a committee was formed under the chairmanship of George F.F.

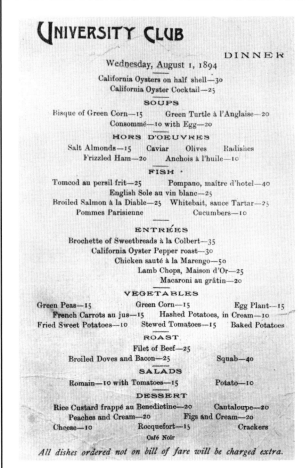

UNIVERSITY CLUB

DINNER

Wednesday, August 1, 1894

California Oysters on half shell—30
California Oyster Cocktail—25

SOUPS

Bisque of Green Corn—15   Green Turtle à l'Anglaise—20
Consommé—10 with Egg—20

HORS D'OEUVRES

Salt Almonds—15   Caviar   Olives   Radishes
Frizzled Ham—20   Anchois à l'huile—10

FISH

Tomcod au persil frit—25   Pompano, maître d'hotel—40
English Sole au vin blanc—25
Broiled Salmon à la Diable—25   Whitebait, sauce Tartar—25
Pommes Parisienne   Cucumbers—10

ENTRÉES

Brochette of Sweetbreads à la Colbert—35
California Oyster Pepper roast—30
Chicken sauté à la Marengo—50
Lamb Chops, Maison d'Or—25
Macaroni au grâtin—20

VEGETABLES

Green Peas—15   Green Corn—15   Egg Plant—15
French Carrots au jus—15   Hashed Potatoes, in Cream—10
Fried Sweet Potatoes—10   Stewed Tomatoes—15   Baked Potatoes

ROAST

Filet of Beef—25
Broiled Doves and Bacon—25   Squab—40

SALADS

Romain—10 with Tomatoes—15   Potato—10

DESSERT

Rice Custard frappé au Benedictine—20   Cantaloupe—20
Peaches and Cream—20   Figs and Cream—20
Cheese—10   Roequefort—15   Crackers
Café Noir

All dishes ordered not on bill of fare will be charged extra.

A Club's menu in early years. Per-item prices were given, contrary to today's practice.

RIGHT: *This early bill for $28.25, rendered to the Reverend Arthur Crosby, includes a printed legend regarding liability for the charges of lady guests. Like several early members, Crosby lived in San Rafael.*

wife. It later passed into the hands of Club member Robert L. Coleman "an earnest and popular member...who, while on an automobile tour of Eastern Europe, was slain by brigands in Albania".

The house was in need of repair and redecoration: Blaisdell described it as a "rather stolid mid-Victorian building". Architect Clinton Day and new member Page Brown (now most remembered for designing the Ferry Building) volunteered their services to renovate and improve 722 Sutter. Day had responsibility for the exterior and Brown acted as interior decorator. The result of their labors was described by Blaisdell as "a home of dignity and harmony" for the Club, with a "lighter character" than it had previously possessed.[20]

Of all the improvements made to the house, the best remembered were the stained glass oriels designed and created by Bruce Porter, each panel depicting the arms or other emblem of a university or college. Blaisdell was to recall them as "colorful and delightful works of art". They were so highly prized that when the time came for the Club to build a new clubhouse, similar ornamentation was installed.[21]

A Peek Inside

In 1898 or 1899, future member I.F. Barreda Sherman, then only a child of six or seven, was taken to the Sutter Street clubhouse for lunch and was greatly impressed.[22] "There was a lounge, a dining room, a domino room...and many bedrooms because many of the Club members then lived at the Club...." He remembered that the dining room was dark green and that a *somelier,* who wore "a leather apron and ...had the keys to the wine cellar hung around his neck", was responsible for the wine service. Most of all, however, he was impressed by a servant:

who went around with a baron of beef in a rolling cart, which he carried [sic] around and

Harrison. Soon, a two story "Victorian" at 722 Sutter Street (between Taylor and Jones) was identified which seemed to answer the Club's needs.[19] Later, several other clubs clustered in this area, including the Bohemian, the Francisca and the Metropolitan.

The house had been the residence of "Phil" Caduc, an early San Francisco brickmaker, pilot commissioner, and well-known yachting enthusiast. By the time the Club decided to lease the house, it was owned by William T. Coleman, the famous organizer of San Francisco's Committee of Vigilance in 1856 and 1877. According to Blaisdell, Coleman had purchased the house as an investment for his

UNIVERSITY CLUB
722 SUTTER ST.

San Francisco, Dec. 4, 1897.

Rev. T. Crosby

To UNIVERSITY CLUB Dr.

To Dues $

" Cards signed Oct 23   2 8 25

" Room

" Messenger Service

" Account rendered

"

" Ch. A.C. 22.50

" G.E. 5.75

"

✓ $ 28 25

Received Payment,

Secretary.

[N. B.—Under Article XVIII of the By-Laws, monthly dues are payable in advance at the Secretary's office of the Club, together with any indebtedness incurred during the previous month, and are delinquent on the 25th day of the current month, when notice of such delinquency is given. Delinquent members are not allowed to incur any further debt in the Club until the amount of such delinquent dues and indebtedness is paid. Members remaining delinquent one month after notice of delinquency, may be suspended or dismissed from the Club by the Board of Directors.

Under House Rule No. 11, all ladies' accounts are payable before the 25th day of the month following that during which such debts were contracted; and unless so paid shall be then charged to the account of the members by whom the ladies were introduced.]

each guest said what piece he wanted. The waiter had on a tall white cap and a white apron, and he had a carving knife attached to chains which were [in turn] attached to a belt around his waist. He would sharpen the knife on the steel and then he would get you a piece of beef.[23]

As today, a high standard of dining was a Club priority; San Francisco's many commercial establishments gave the Club's kitchen stiff competition. A dinner menu dated August 1, 1894 gives some idea of the range of delicacies available and, contrary to today's practice, gives prices for each item.

In view of the controversy which arose ninety years later regarding the admission of women, it is worth noting that among the first additions made to the original clubhouse were a ladies' reception room and dining room in the front basement. Although ladies were not permitted to become members, their presence as guests was so much taken for granted that the early printed invoices of the Club included a paragraph specifically dealing with a member's liability for settling the debts incurred by his female guests.

The opening of 722 Sutter as a clubhouse had a good effect. At once, Blaisdell records, the members grouped themselves as "glassmates, tablemates, baseball teams, trap shots, polo players, card tournaments, domino bouts, all leading to...good fellowship". Membership grew rapidly, requiring expansion into the house next door on the west side, so that the Club acquired nine additional bedrooms. In 1893, the front of the original house was extended toward the street line in order to view the passing female parade and play a hand at the same time. On the second floor, a library was installed which, according to Blaisdell, "was a benediction to the users and a revelation to visitors".

Notes

1. Known initially as the Chronicle and later the De Young building.

2. The San Francisco Harvard Club was organized on January 15, 1874. *Bluebook* (1889), p. 268. It was without premises of its own and therefore not comparable to the Harvard Club of New York. As the meeting of July 17 demonstrated, it was not strictly an *alumni* association; many of the men who attended were not of Harvard. But at this time Harvard accounted for a much higher proportion of the total of college educated men than it does today. By 1890, Harvard had graduated 18,200 students in its entire history and had 9,947 living *alumni*. Both numbers are far higher than those reported by any other U.S. institution. *World Almanac*, 1890-91, pp. 144-145.

3. Thomas was born in Worcester, Massachusetts on September 5, 1853. According to his biography in *San Francisco: Its Builders Past and Present* (1913), he came from a well-known New England family with roots going back to colonial times. His grandfather Isiah Thomas was "a warm personal friend" of Benjamin Franklin, founded the famous satirical publication *Spy*, and helped to found the American Antiquarian Association.

Grandson Thomas entered Harvard at age 15, married Emma Gay at age 18 in 1875, and after graduation with both an A.B. and LL.B., came to San Francisco in 1877.

Thomas, admitted to the California bar, was a man of great professional ability, social status and commitment to the welfare of San Francisco. He became an expert in corporate law and was one of the organizers of the California Title Insurance Company. He also formed and became the first President of the California Fruit Canners' Association. He was a trustee of the Home for the Feeble Minded.

Perhaps his greatest achievement came during the dark days just after the San Francisco earthquake and fire of 1906. Four German insurance companies had refused to indemnify the losses of clients of some sixty law firms. In the fall of 1906 Thomas and Oscar Sutro traveled to Germany and secured $7,000,000 from the insurers.

As a clubman, Thomas was not only associated with the Harvard and University Clubs, but with the Commonwealth and Bohemian Clubs as well.

4. Entertainments went on late a hundred years ago, and this event was not unusual. When, in 1902, the Sutter Club of Sacramento extended the hours of its Wine Room until midnight, "Club revenues increased immediately". Timothy F. Comstock, *The Sutter Club: One Hundred Years* (Sacramento: The Sutter Club, 1989), p. 47. (Cited hereafter as Comstock 1989).

5. Wheeler practised law with John Hays Hammond, and eventually became vice-president and managing director of the Mt. Whitney Power Company.

Wheeler had affiliations with other clubs: he was a founder of the Burlingame Country Club and secretary of the Pacific Union Club for a number of years.

6. Article II, s. 1 of the original by-laws allowed as members only those "who shall have been regularly connected as a student with a university or college of recognized standing" or those holding honorary degrees. But by 1903, this by-law had been amended to allow up to seventy-five members who did not meet such criteria. Since the passage of this amendment, it has not been a prerequisite of membership that a candidate have attended a college or university.

The original by-law provision is not easy to reconcile with the fact that some of the founder members seem not to have had any college or university education.

Graduation from a college or university has never been a requirement for membership.

7. The University Club of New York was among the earliest, founded in 1865.

An article entitled "The Rise and Progress of the Club", published in 1884, gushed:

Every large American city now has several of them [clubs], and in New York they are almost as numerous as in London. Some of the New York clubs have a style of unparalleled magnificence. There has always been a marked tendency toward club life in San Francisco.

–*Social Manual for San Francisco and Oakland* (San Francisco: the City Publishing Co., 1884), pp. 164-168.

8. San Francisco had not only a Merchants' Club (known as the Merchants' League until 1888), but several clubs of the same sort under other names. For example, the Concordia-Argonaut Club's self-description was as follows: "It is the principal Jewish society in the city, and composed chiefly of wholesale merchants". *Bluebook* (1889), p. 179.

9. Another aspect of the duplication of name was that when members of a city's University Club relocated, they often applied for membership of the University Club in their new city. And the coincidence of name was also a factor with father and son: Frederick O. Johnson, President of the San Francisco University Club from 1971 to 1972, joined because his father had been a member of the University Club of Los Angeles.

10. Carolan was raised in Sacramento and came to San Francisco to open a dried fruit store. Two years after the formation of the Club, Carolan had the good luck – or good sense - to marry Harriet Pullman, heiress to the Pullman railroad fortune. When her father George Mortimer Pullman died in 1897, the couple became fabulously wealthy. Carolan became a well-known clubman, especially at the Burlingame Country Club, near which he and his wife built the huge "Carolands Chateau", which still stands as a now almost forgotten monument to the San Francisco Peninsula's age of elegance.

11. Blaisdell said that Carlin was a product of the United States Naval Academy, but this is incorrect. According to the *Register of Commissioned Officers of the Navy* (1864), he entered the service on July 23, 1864, but was not at the Academy.

12. Eells' father, James Eells, was a prominent Presbyterian minister.

13. The inscription on his statue outside City Hall describes him as "leader of the California bar, learned, eloquent, able, fearless advocate, courteous foe".

14. Sherwood and Sherwood were the Pacific Coast agents for Moet et Chandon champagne, Bass ale, Epps' cocoa, Schlitz beer, Ross's Belfast ginger ale, a variety of Kentucky whiskies and various wines. Sherwood was probably a popular early member.

15. Although Blaisdell's history attributes an education at Columbia University to Smedberg, his biography in volume 2 of *San Francisco: Its Builders Past and Present* (1913), pp. 159-160, does not and Columbia has no record of his enrollment in any department of the University.

Smedberg had a valiant Civil War record, serving in the Union interest. While an aide to General Charles Griffin of the First Division of the Fifth Army Corps during the Battle of the Wilderness in 1864 he lost his right foot in an explosion. Nevertheless, after recuperation he returned to active service in 1865 as Captain of the "Bloody Fourteenth" stationed in San Francisco.

He was a member of the Bohemian and Union League Clubs.

16. Symmes had reached his junior year at Harvard in 1866 when he decided to volunteer for the navy. He served as an engineer in the South Pacific squadron on the U.S.S. Dakota and other ships. After being discharged from the navy he came to San Francisco to work as a salesman for the Thomas Day Company, manufacturers of gas fixtures and supplies. In that capacity, he met and married Miss Anna Day, his boss's daughter, in 1871: by 1886 he was president of the company.

Symmes served on the Board of Education between 1894-95 and was on the Board of Visitors to the United States Naval Academy in 1899. In 1900 he returned to Harvard and completed his B.S. degree. Returning to San Francisco thereafter, he became president of the Merchants' Association from 1901 to 1908, in which capacity he assumed a crucial role in relief work and the rebuilding of San Francisco following the disaster of 1906.

Besides the University Club, *San Francisco: Its Builders Past and Present* (1913) lists his other affiliations as the Republican party, and the Harvard, Unitarian and Chit-Chat Clubs.

17. Blaisdell recorded that in "the era of goodwill" (the turn of the century), "the act of dining and after dinner speaking flowered...."

18. But the age of plentiful domestic servants is not wholly to blame; some of today's members remain likewise innocent of the culinary arts.

19. 722 Sutter Street is not an address that exists any longer. The site is now occupied by the Whitehall apartments, next to the Canterbury Hotel.

20. Page Brown's interior ornamentation was augmented by the members' gifts and loans. A loan which may have been the very start of the Club's collection of stuffed animals was one by George H.P. Hill "of three Caribou heads", for which the board thanked him on July 23, 1901.

21. Porter's work was destroyed in the earthquake and fire of 1906, but members liked it so much that new stained glasses were commissioned for the clubhouse built in 1909.

22. A few years later, he would have been barred under House Rule 21, providing: "No children shall be introduced into the Club House". *By-Laws* 1903, p. 62.

23. The rolling cart carrying a baron of beef no longer survives at the Club: but the House of Prime Rib and a few other venerable bay area restaurants still maintain the tradition.

CHAPTER 2

Paying for Pleasure

Finances and Board Responsibilities

From the beginning, the Board's major preoccupation was finance.[1] In the euphoria of creating the Club, relatively little thought had been given to its long-term financing. At its inception, the Club had no source of income other than its members and no reserves[2] and the long-term financial needs of the enterprise were scarcely considered by its founders.

The original members subscribed the Club's legally required capital, paid dues plus a few special assessments, and made modest gifts (almost all in services or in kind rather than money), but these sources were not enough to provide for the long-term. By the turn of the century, the Board had found it necessary to appeal to members to make loans to the Club by buying its bonds; the President periodically conducted a lottery to determine which of the bondholders should be paid back first.[3] The Club accumulated any current surplus at the Hibernia Bank, but it was not the Board's practice in the early years to seek commercial loans.

Related to its duty to secure the financial health of the Club was the necessity of seeing that members paid their bills. One of the earliest surviving entries in the Club's Minute Book records that: "The Secretary was instructed to write to several delinquents of long standing, and to remind them that action in their cases would be forthcoming at the next meeting". Those to be contacted were then listed. The problem — not unique to the University Club — has often recurred down the years.[4]

Another major responsibility of the Board was all matters related to Club employees. It employed Club managers and, in an era long before collective bargaining, set wages for all employees. The earliest surviving record of a major action taken by the Board is that of December 27, 1900 when it approved the recommendation of Director Dirwell Hewitt to hire L.E. Marting as "a manager for this Club" at $100 per month.[5] A month later, President James M. Seawell appointed Secretary-Treasurer G.L. Rathbone and Director J.K. Moffitt to work with the new manager in arranging uniforms for the Club's employees.

So began a parade of managers whose turnover has been rather high. Notwithstanding that the manager's monthly salary was raised to $175 in July 1902, it was necessary to hire a new manager, H. Barker, in June of 1904 (at a lesser salary of $125 per month), and within two years he was replaced by Stanley Hudd.

In the early years the Board not only reported upon the Club's financial condition at the annual meeting (held, in accordance with its by-laws, in May), but also proposed, or designated a member to

UNIVERSITY CLUB

Dinner to the Visiting Professors of the Summer School of the University of California.

SAN FRANCISCO, July 26th, 1902.

On Friday evening, August 1st, the University Club will give a dinner in honor of the visiting Professors of the Summer School of the University of California. President Wheeler has brought to the Coast men of high attainments and brilliant records.

Those of our members who were fortunate enough to hear the after-dinner talks of the visiting Professors last year will recall a most delightful and enjoyable evening.

The following gentlemen have been invited to be present as guests of the Club:

CHARLES SEARS BALDWIN,
Asst. Prof. of Rhetoric in Yale University

JAMES MARK BALDWIN,
Prof. of Psychology in Princeton University

ROBERT A. HARPER,
Prof. of Botany in University of Michigan

JAMES ARNOLD HENRY,
Prof. of Agriculture in University of Wisconsin

ARTHUR LACHMAN,
Prof. of Chemistry in University of Oregon

ERNEST G. MERRITT,
Asst. Prof. of Physics in Cornell University

JOSIAH ROYCE,
Prof. of Philosphy in Harvard University

FREDERICK NEWTON SCOTT,
Jr. Prof. of Rhetoric in University of Michigan

F. LOUIS SOLDAN,
Supt. of Instruction in St. Louis, Missouri

HENRY MORSE STEPHENS,
Prof. of History in University of California

You are earnestly requested to aid us by your presence in extending the hospitality of the Club to these University men.

The price of the dinner will be $1.50 per plate, including red and white wines.

It is important that the enclosed postal be returned to the Secretary not later than the 31st inst.

F. H. WHEELAN,
President.

H. D. PILLSBURY,
Secretary.

LEFT: *An announcement of the Club's dinner to the University of California's summer school faculty, 1902.*

propose, a Club program for the following year. The annual meeting of 1905 was memorable in this respect, as member James D. Phelan, former crusading mayor of San Francisco (1897-1901) and future United States Senator (1915-1921) addressed the 31 members present "on the social affairs of the Club".

Recruiting New Members

Once the initial enthusiasm to form the Club had worn off, it soon became apparent that attracting new members was at least as important a Board function as keeping the existing members happy: the financial health of the enterprise depended on it.[6] The Club had a distinguished roster from the start and desirable members were constantly being proposed for membership,[7] but a Club needs new blood. Hence, at a specially called meeting on June 4, 1901, the Board appointed a special purpose committee[8] to obtain and peruse a "list of College graduates with a view to increasing the Club's membership". This paid off. The President was able to report by October, 1902:

> The Club has reached the 500 mark for the first time in its history; the membership having increased since May 1, 1902, from 460 to 505 — members to the number of 108 having been elected or reinstated during that time. The present outlook promises that the membership will be materially increased in the near future.

This upbeat news was rounded out with the conclusion: "All need of an assessment is happily eliminated".

As part of its strategy, the Club attempted to cement its university connections by inviting not only recent graduates but also their professors to join. At a special meeting on September 6, 1901, Article XVII, section 3 was added to the by-laws, waiving admission fees for instructors at the University of California or Stanford as long as they were "not

practicing any other profession for emolument".[9] Such members were exempted from assessments and paid reduced dues; while dues for regular members were $7.50, instructors paid only $3.75 per month if they were residents and $2.50 if non-resident.[10]

Other manifestations of the Club's eagerness to capitalize upon its special relationship with the academic world were the dinners it gave in honor of the visiting faculty of the University of California's summer school, most of whom were from distinguished institutions elsewhere. The announcement of such an event in 1902 survives, reminding members that "the after-dinner talks of the visiting Professors last year" provided "a most delightful and enjoyable evening"; evidently the guests of honor had to sing for their supper. Besides this attraction, the occasion gave Club members who had been educated in the east — who still predominated — the opportunity to renew acquaintance with some of their erstwhile mentors.

Locomotive Smith

The Club's close connection with both the University of California and Stanford led to its being appointed arbiter of a volatile controversy between the two schools in the fall of 1902. A few days before the Big Game, Stanford questioned the eligibility of "Locomotive Smith", one of California's great footballers, to play. I.F. Barreda Sherman explained: "Those were the days of push and grunt on the football field...and he (the Locomotive) was pretty good at pushing and grunting...."[11] A quick resolution of this dispute was direly needed and the Club was asked to settle the matter. In order to do so, President Fairfax Wheelan appointed a committee made up of one member from every college represented in the Club. According to Nathaniel Blaisdell, this group met for two nights in succession, deliberating "until the midnight hours". After hearing testimony and weighing the evidence, they "voted unanimously against the 'Locomotive'". California's supporters were incensed; their slogan became "Remember Smith".

To the collective relief of Club members, the Locomotive's replacement, Bobby Sherman (no relation to member Barreda), fielded the opening kickoff and, behind "the great" Ovie Overall, ran ninety-five yards for a touchdown. As Blaisdell commented, "California won, and the University Club was forgiven".

The recognition of instructors as a special category of membership having been a success, in January 1903 the Board recommended that the Club offer selected honorary memberships and specifically on January 27 agreed that, if this suggestion were approved, the botanist Luther Burbank would be invited to accept this distinction. At the annual meeting, the members approved and Burbank became the Club's first honorary member.

In April 1902, a different kind of initiative was taken by the Board to enhance the benefits of membership, when it approved the first reciprocal arrangements by which members could obtain guest privileges at the University Clubs of Cleveland, Detroit and Pittsburgh. This was the beginning of a network which would ultimately extend worldwide, and provide homes-away-from-home for traveling members. Its original modest beginning was so successful that a "League" of University Clubs was proposed by the University Club of Buffalo and on August 8, 1902, Director Knox Maddox was appointed to sit on the League's executive committee. The Club's membership in this League is particularly interesting, because as explained in chapter 1, the choice of the name "University Club" was spontaneous and independent and did not connote any tie to such clubs elsewhere. Thus, the modern network of reciprocal clubs has its origin in the coincidence of a shared name.

The Fate of the Ladies

Another sort of attempt to accommodate members' wishes did not fare so well. Almost as soon as the Club had occupied 722 Sutter, facilities for ladies had been provided, and for the first few years they had been regularly utilized. By 1901, however, the Board had become concerned with the lack of utilization of the "ladies' restaurant". Board member H.D. Pillsbury lamented on July 23: "that there was a seeming negligence on the part of members to take advantage

of the House Rule allowing the issuance of the two cards extending privileges of the ladies' restaurant". Later that year, in an effort to increase patronage, members were allowed additional "special Visitors' Cards", good for twenty days, for "ladies not residents of San Francisco". The decline in the popularity of the ladies' dining room was never reversed and may have been a factor in the Club's later restrictions upon the admission of female guests.

The Pre-1906 Search for a New Home

Although the Club acquired its present premises in the wake of the 1906 earthquake, several plans to move from 722 Sutter Street had been proposed before then.

There were at least two reasons for this. Initially, the seeds of impermanence were sewn by the fact that the Club did not own, but only leased, 722 Sutter. There had always been sentiment in favor of owning a building, underlying which was a desire for a custom-designed clubhouse instead of a mere conversion of an existing structure.[12]

Also, by 1903, the Club had been the victim of its own success; even after the expansion of 722 Sutter into the house next door, the premises were inadequate to the needs of the membership. This fact was informally recognized, but did not become a live issue until the annual meeting of 1903 at which William B. Bourn, the great entrepreneur who became the last private owner of San Francisco's water supply, was elected as the Club's President. Foremost on his agenda was the building of a new, larger clubhouse. In furtherance of that aim, an architectural competition was held to select the designer of the proposed new premises.[13] The winner was Willis Polk, then San Francisco's foremost architect. On October 20, Bourn appointed a special committee, comprising himself, Secretary-Treasurer Knox Maddox and Director George Lent, to oversee the planning for the new facility.

By March, 1904, great progress had been made. A potential site had been identified on the northeast corner of Van Ness Avenue and Sutter Street, which

the Board recommended.[14] On March 23, an evening meeting was held to act on the Board's recommendation at which 58 members were present. With the aid of many proxies, the Board's motion in favor of the Van Ness project carried. But nothing like a consensus existed. William Denman moved an amendment to the Board's resolution "that the matter of the proposed change in residence of the Club be discussed at this meeting and be referred to a committee to report at another meeting to be held not later than one month from this meeting". Although the amendment failed and therefore the Board's motion passed, there was substantial opposition; the vote was 102 in favor, 65 opposed.

Bourn himself was troubled by the large number of votes against the Board's proposal and before the meeting ended he suggested that a special committee be formed to report on alternatives to the Board's plan, in the hope that its findings would promote "greater unanimity among the members". Six members[15] were appointed to this committee, none of whom sat on the Board.

At the next meeting of the Board on March 25, the committee was asked "to harmonize the opposing

The clubhouse that never was: the front elevation of Willis Polk's 1904 design for the University Club when it was considering a site on the corner of Van Ness Avenue and Sutter Street.

elements of the Club" — a task, in this context as in many others, easier stated than achieved. It rapidly became clear that for the time being harmonious acquiescence in the Board's Van Ness proposal was not in the cards. Indeed, only three weeks later, the special committee reported back with a recommendation quite contrary to the Board's, abandoning the Van Ness proposal in favor of a site at Stockton and Pine. The Board reversed its previous recommendation and endorsed that of the special committee on condition that the site could be obtained for $100,000 or less and approved a search for a loan of $300,000 for the building project.

Some insight into the Board's reasoning can be obtained from a most important stipulation it attached to the new building project: the new building must include fifty bedrooms. Polk's plans made provision for only thirty-two. This reflected two important concerns. First, there was heavy demand by members for residential tenancies within the Club. Second, rentals from such rooms, which leased out at from $25 to $50 a month, would be an important source of revenue for the future which, the Board believed, could guarantee that regular members' dues would be kept at or below $7.50 a month.[16] So determined was the Board to capture such revenue that it resolved that if the Club had not found a new permanent facility by the time the lease on 722 Sutter expired, it would lease temporary quarters which *did* have fifty bedrooms and, to compensate members for the inconvenience of temporary facilities, reduce dues to $5.00 per month.

However, some of the opposition to the proposed move was not merely to the particular site under study, but to any move whatever; members against a move circulated a letter which persuaded the Board, at its April 29 meeting, to give up its endeavor.[17] Because the Directors believed that "the successful accomplishment of any such plan" required the support of practically all classes of membership, they announced their relinquishment of the quest for a new clubhouse and voted to submit their resignations at the upcoming annual meeting, noting, however, that: "for the encouragement of that spirit of harmony and cooperation which the Board believes is essential to the Club's welfare, each member of the Board hereby declares himself in favor of a plan for a permanent site and clubhouse that may hereafter be presented and that may meet with the approval of a substantial majority of the members of the Club".

At the annual meeting on May 5, 1905, the Directors' resignations were accepted and a new Board was voted into office under President Thomas Magee. Its mandate was to abandon plans for a new clubhouse and concentrate upon the upgrading of 722 Sutter Street. In consequence, the Club's lease on 722 Sutter was renewed for ten years beginning January 1, 1906, with an option for a further five years. As events turned out, the Club enjoyed possession under this renewal for less than four months and was thereafter forced to find a new abode. In the meantime, improvements continued on Sutter Street. A circular to members of March 1, 1905 announced that the little-used "women's department" was closed, "thereby effecting a saving of $101.50 per month rental".

Notes

1. How the Board functioned during the first ten years cannot be exactly ascertained because the Minutes of its meetings 1890-1900 were destroyed in the earthquake and fire of 1906. However, Minutes from December 1900 on, except for 1942-52, survive.

2. A practice developed by which initiation fees were put into a capital account, but this was not mandated by the Club's by-laws.

3. If a bondholder died, his estate was paid back as soon as it was feasible.

4. See, e.g., the Club's *Annual Report* (1909), p.6, remarking that dues delinquencies were "out of all proportion for a Club of this size". And for the parallel experience of another club only 90 miles to the east of San Francisco, see Comstock 1989, pp.112, 173-174.

An allied problem which would plague future Boards also surfaced early – that of missing Club properties. For example, the Minutes of February 26, 1901 note that:

> A communication was read from Mr Leverance relative to the disappearance from the Library of the volume of *Burke's Peerage*. Referred to the Committee on Literature and Art with the recommendation that the books on the shelves be checked with the Catalogue.

In later years, copies of *Playboy* disappeared from the library more frequently than *Burke's Peerage*. A solution was found by taking the magazine out of general circulation and putting it on special reserve with the fourth-floor bartender.

5. It is not known whether the Club employed a manager before this.

6. As the historian of Sacramento's Sutter Club put it, when revenues went down "new blood was the proven tonic". Comstock 1989, p.100.

7. An example was William Keith, the famous western artist, who, although not a charter member, became a member in the Club's early years. To him belongs the credit for making to the Club its single most valuable gift: an original landscape which today adorns the fourth floor lounge. It has a large tree in the foreground. Henry Hardy described that painting as one of Keith's "best known", but in this he erred. Far from being well-known, it was unknown enough to be hailed as a discovery by a professional appraiser in 1989 and the standard works on Keith do not mention it.

8. Comprised of founding President Thomas, Secretary-Treasurer M.N. Wilson and Director J.K. Moffitt.

9. This caveat was almost certainly inserted with the faculty of the University of California's original law school (Hastings College of the Law) and its medical school in mind: many of their faculty were practitioners.

   Experience soon showed that the restriction of this category to the University of California and Stanford did not make sense in a Club in which *alumni* of east coast schools still predominated. At the annual meeting of May 13, 1902, the membership voted to widen it to include instructors at any college or university approved by the Board.

10. On February 24, 1905, the by-laws were amended again to lower the resident instructors' dues to $3.25 per month.

11. Sherman, whose father was on the faculty of the University of California medical school, witnessed the game. He recalled that it was played on neutral territory in San Francisco, at a field "about where Lake Street runs across Park Presidio".

12. A Board communication to members dated March 10, 1904 declared: "Your Directors deem it wise and desirable that the Club should own its permanent home".

13. Architectural competitions were common as the west coast developed; the Club was following the example of the University of California which, when Mrs Phoebe Hearst pledged the necessary funds, had held a similar competition "open to all the architects of the world" for the design of 28 buildings on the Berkeley campus.

14. Van Ness Avenue was being touted as San Francisco's premier "boulevard" and it was expected to become a fashionable area.

   The site was that now occupied by the Regency I and II movie theaters. Had the Club located there, it would have been only two blocks from the Concordia-Argonaut Club, which has been on Van Ness Avenue since 1893. *Bluebook* (1893-94), p.100.

15. F.J. Symmes, W.B. Story, Jr., J.S. Severance, A. Stillman, J.K. Moffitt and J.A. Wright.

16. When 800 Powell Street was in the course of construction, the President predicted that "the rent of the building should be more than met from the rent of rooms to members". *Annual Report*, May 11, 1909, p.8.

17. Director M.F. Michael explained that "this Board finds that said plan is strenuously opposed by a minority of the members of the Club" and that "the criticisms and suggestions offer to this Board no sound reason for modifying its original plan in any essential particular but leave this Board impressed with the futility of any further attempt to enlist the cordial and active support of any considerable portion of said minority to the said plan". Many subsequent Boards have felt the same way about many subsequent issues.

CHAPTER 3

Earthquake and Relocation

Despite the mandate given to President Thomas Magee to treat 722 Sutter as the Club's home for the foreseeable future, fate was to decree otherwise. The clubhouse was completely destroyed on April 18, 1906 by the earthquake and its resulting fire. By one of those strange twists which make history fascinating, Magee (who turned out to be the longest-serving President in the Club's history) guided the Club towards a completely new home - the exact opposite of the mandate on which he was elected.

Club historian Nathaniel Blaisdell felt that the earthquake "ended the Club's adolescence". On the fateful day of April 18, Harold Wheeler, the Club's Secretary, was on hand just before flames consumed it. He managed to come away with a few of the Club's records and its prized Keith landscape which, with great presence of mind, he cut out from its frame. Apart from these salvages, the Club suffered a total loss and nothing else is known to have been saved; Blaisdell reveals that "the insurance had been allowed to lapse and the loss was complete".[1]

After the earthquake, the first Board meeting took place in June of 1906, the May annual meeting having been postponed by necessity. Its first sad business was acceptance of 25 resignations from members who had been wiped out by the disaster.

At the annual meeting which took place on July 26, the 31 members present agreed to assess each member $50 to pay off debts on the clubhouse amounting to some $15,000. Recognizing that hard times lay ahead, they lowered monthly dues to $4.00.

Temporary Quarters

The immediate problem of rehousing the Club was solved with surprising ease through the generosity of a member, Dr Kasper Pischel, who made available for an initial term of one year a "double house" at 1815-1817 California Street as the University Club's temporary headquarters.[2] This property had remained undamaged by the disaster of April 18 because, being west of Franklin Street, it had not been reached by the conflagration following the earthquake. The Board accepted Dr Pischel's offer with alacrity. Although the Board could not know it, the decision was a harbinger of the future: the Club would ever after dwell on California Street.[3]

Notwithstanding that Dr Pischel had done the Club a great favor, the arrangement by which the "double house" was taken was flawed in two respects. First, Dr Pischel had invited the Club to occupy part of a building in which he and his wife made their home: this was a formula for friction.[4] Second, he assumed that the Club's occupancy would last for a year at most, a prognostication that turned out to be much too modest.

To make the California Street house more

Eadweard Muybridge's 1878 panoramic view from the top of the Mark Hopkins mansion showing (bottom left) Leland Stanford's stable on the site now occupied by the University Club. As the picture attests, Stanford's stable was grander than many of California Street's dwellings.

Muybridge (1830-1904) was born in and died in England: but much of his life was spent in the American west. His photographs of old San Francisco are regarded as the best made of any American city of the era.

clublike, the Board installed a billiard table and a piano. The latter immediately exposed the shortcomings of Dr Pischel's attempt to accommodate both his family and the Club; the piano became a source of irritation to Mrs Pischel, who asked that it be removed. It was not a sign of harmony that at its meeting of October 9, 1907 (when the Club had already overstayed its original one-year welcome), the Board declined to honor her request.

This was by no means her only ground of complaint: some of the Club functions were overlubricated. At the Christmas dinner held on December 27, 1907, it was reported to the Board on the following January 8, "the conduct of certain members...had been the subject of criticism both by members...and other persons". And even without a Club function, some members were frequently drunk. The Board noted of Mr. R.C. Van Fleet:

this member came in about one A.M. September 29, 1908 while intoxicated, and with a stranger also intoxicated. They were put to bed, and in the morning the stranger left with the shoes and hat of Mr Thomas and other properties....[I]t had been a habit of Mr Van

Fleet to be at the Club generally *only* when in that condition. On motion duly seconded, Mr Severance was instructed to replace or refund values of articles taken.[5]

The term of the Club's original lease on California Street turned out not to be enough. Since after one year there, nothing decisive had been done to secure new quarters, Dr Pischel agreed to extend the lease until August of 1908. It may be surmised that by providing the Club with a convenient short-term solution to its accommodation problem, Dr Pischel had unwittingly forestalled urgent action to secure the longer-term future of the Club. As Blaisdell put it, everyone had to realise that "old San Francisco was gone forever": but in the absence of immediate urgency, it was not easy for the membership to agree what the shape of the future should be.

It was not that the question was ignored; the trouble was that the California Street incumbency gave the Club the luxury of an indecisiveness which, if it had remained homeless, it would not have enjoyed. Neither was it that the location really suited members; the *Annual Report* of 1909 observed that it had "become more and more inconvenient as business returned to the downtown district".

A panorama of the devastation of the 1906 earthquake.

Many sites were considered beginning in January of 1907; the problem was one of an *embarras de richesse*. In the next eighteen months at least seven sites would be seriously considered by the Board.[6] On January 29, 1907, the Board began its search with an "informal discussion" of the desirability of locating the Club on the "California Street hill" or in the neighborhood of its former location on Sutter Street. Ironically, in view of the Club's ultimate decision, only one director, J.S. Severance, favored "the hill". The rest wanted a site near the old clubhouse.[7]

House Hunting

Few of the details of the Board's search have any general interest. The task was a frustrating one: during a period of one month beginning on August 7, 1907, the Board tried to meet on six different occasions without mustering a quorum; it seems likely that morale was low and tempers frayed. But when finally the Board did meet, it was getting close to the end of its quest.

By September 17, the site being most seriously considered was one on the northwest corner of Powell and Post (on Union Square), where E.W. Hopkins proposed to construct a building in which the University Club could lease the two top floors, including 35 to 40 bedrooms and other facilities, for

$1,500 a month.[8] This location satisfied the demand of the majority of the Board for a new site close to 722 Sutter, and Directors W. Wharton Thurston and A.J. Dibblee were asked to investigate, which they did well into 1908; the Hopkins site almost became the Club's new home and remained a prime contender until the end.

Early in the New Year, while Directors Thurston and Dibblee investigated the Hopkins proposal, a new possibility emerged. At the Board's meeting of January 14, 1908, discussion began of the possibility of buying the stables of the old Stanford mansion on the corner of California and Powell Streets.[9] The earlier preference for a site elsewhere than the California Street hill evaporated, or at least turned out not to be insurmountable.

Three days later, Directors J.S.Severance and William Denman reported that the owners of the stable site, the trustees of the Leland Stanford Jr. University, were "inclined to entertain some proposition from the Club in regard to the construction of a building". The Board acted swiftly, and at a special meeting called on January 22, envisioned the construction of a $100,000 building at the corner of California and Powell that the Club would lease from the trustees. Thus, in only eight days the Club's destiny had been crystalized.

But the Board had chased enough will o' the wisps and was not carried away by the prospect of the Nob Hill lease; it continued to pursue the Hopkins proposal and on March 16, authorized Directors Thurston and Dibblee to bargain for a tenancy at this site. The Minutes of the Board's March 22 meeting are explicit about the benefits of its two-pronged approach; continuing negotiations with both parties gave the Club an alternative if one fell through.

For several more weeks, it was nip and tuck between the Hopkins and Stanford proposals. On April 2, the Board found that if the Stanford proposal was to be pursued further, the Club would have to spend money on preliminary planning without any guarantee that it would come to fruition. Director Dibblee, one of the two responsible for investigating the Hopkins proposal, objected to this on the ground that agreement with E.W. Hopkins was imminent. The result of his objection, however, was not to

dissuade the Board, but only that it authorized similar preliminary expenses on the Hopkins site as well.[10]

When the Board met again on April 7, the estimate for constructing a clubhouse on the Stanford site had risen from $100,000 to $150,000 and it therefore had to ascertain whether the Stanford trustees were willing to increase their commitment to the project by 50%. In the meantime, to entice the Club, Hopkins offered it another floor in his building (making three in all). Recognizing that Hopkins had negotiated with the Club in a generous spirit, the Board voted on April 11 that, if it ultimately did not take Hopkins' proposition, it would reimburse him $800 of his design expenses. Then, the Woodruff Company, the contractors for Hopkins' building, informed the Club, as a further expression of goodwill, that it would pay the $800 to Hopkins, so that the Club would have no need to reimburse him.

A New Home in a Stable

On May 20, 1908, the climax came. With all the Directors present at 4.30 pm at the temporary clubhouse at 1815-1817 California:

> It was moved by Mr Thurston and seconded by Mr Dibblee, that the Board of Directors of the University Club make an offer to Mr E.W. Hopkins to take a ten year lease on the three upper floors of the building proposed to be created on his lot at the northwest corner of Post and Powell Streets, according to the plans and specifications heretofore prepared by the Woodruff Company, at a monthly rental of $1,500, said offer to be subject to the approval of the Club.

The motion failed, with President Magee, Vice-President William B. Bosley and Directors Moffitt, Severance and Denman against it.

A new motion was then made:

> that the Board of Directors adopt the Stanford site and the plans for the building proposed to be erected thereon, heretofore prepared by

Messrs Bliss and Faville, and in accordance with the proposition heretofore submitted to and offered by the trustees of Stanford University, and recommend the same to the Club at the annual meeting for approval and confirmation.

This carried, with only Directors Thurston and Dibblee opposed, but then, in a demonstration of unity and good fellowship, "It was moved by Mr Thurston and seconded by Mr Dibblee, that the recommendation be made unanimous." Now, all that remained was for the membership as a whole to approve the Board's recommendation. It was placed on the agenda of the Club's annual meeting set for May 12, but a quorum was not obtained then or at the first adjourned date of the annual meeting on May 21. Finally, however, on May 28, some sixty members appeared and the resolution to enter into an agreement with the Stanford trustees passed. Then a motion was made by William B. Bourn, who had spent so much of his time as President on similar matters, and seconded by S.B. McNear, to extend thanks "to the President and Board of Directors for their endeavors in finding a permanent home for the Club and for the results accomplished by them". The deed was done!

Building 800 Powell

Once the Club's future was assured, former members such as M.M. O'Shaughnessy and Alfred von der Ropp rejoined, and many new men sought nomination for membership.

The agreement reached with the Stanford trustees was that they would arrange construction of a "class C" building at a cost of between $100,000 and $150,000[11] and lease it to the Club for thirty years at a rent "equal to seven per cent per annum on the cost of the building...and four per cent upon the value of the land".[12] Rent was payable monthly, together with contributions towards a sinking fund which would help the Club purchase the building anytime after the first ten years of the lease. The Club had responsibility for insurance, taxes, utilities and maintenance and could not make any permanent

alterations without the trustees' consent.

Formally the Stanford trustees, not the Club, had responsibility for building a clubhouse, but the Club's wishes were by and large respected and Walter Bliss and William Faville were chosen as architects by mutual agreement. But the trustees were masters of the project, as the letting of the construction contract revealed. Club President Warren Olney, Jr. wanted E. Remington to have it; Remington, eager to have it, even applied to join the Club. But at the Board meeting of October 6, 1908, Olney had to report that the Stanford trustees wished to place the job with the Lewis A. Hicks Company. That was it; a contract with Hicks was signed on October 6, setting a total price of $107,000 plus a $5,000 commission.[13] Only one hitch was encountered during construction: Blaisdell records that a vertical iron girder toppled while the building's steel frame was being erected. It had not been stayed securely enough to resist Nob Hill's high speed winds.

In three particular ways, the Club rapidly took advantage of the opportunity, extended by the agreement with the Stanford trustees, to incur additional indebtedness (up to $125,000) in making improvements. First, it paved "Miles Street" (now known as Miles Court) behind the clubhouse. Second, the Board decided, on October 6, to put all the Club's wiring in conduit "even at some considerable expense". And third, on March 5, 1909, the Board resolved to put a sprinkler system in the kitchen, machine room, stoke room and over the elevator and back stairs. Such additional expenses not added to the Stanford loan were covered by assessments on members.

Another farsighted action of the Board was to obtain a ten-year option to buy the lot next to the Stanford stables from its owner, Mrs Vienna Belle Turner: during the first five years, the price would be $15,000 and during the second a mutually acceptable price. Twenty years after the Club exercised this option, the lot became the site of the squash courts,[14] but the original motive for obtaining the option was to provide the Club with room for a more ambitious "athletic annex". Bliss & Faville actually produced plans for such a facility, which included not only squash courts, but two bowling alleys at a total cost of $9,500. These plans were reviewed by the Board on April 27, 1909, but not adopted because they could not be financed through the Stanford trustees.[15]

Expenditures for the interior of the Club were considerable, among them being:

From the D.N. and E. Walker Company:

rugs and carpets	$3,676
draperies	3,399
furniture	12,242

From the Nathan Dohrman Company:

china	1,542
glassware	772

From Reed and Brown:

silverware	3,846

From D. Samuels Lace House Company:

linen	2,191

From Sherman, Clay and Company:

a Steinway piano	850
Total	$ 28,518

In addition, in March, 1909 the Board approved an expenditure of $5,000 "for the purpose of placing velour on the walls of the living-room" and $1,140 to purchase a range and other "necessary appurtenances" for the kitchen.

While all these arrangements were being approved, Dr Pischel was getting very restless. He had reluctantly agreed to allow the Club to stay on at 1815-1817 California Street until July 1, 1909 when, the President had reported on May 11, "Dr Pischel...has informed us that he will positively require the building". But the new clubhouse was nowhere near complete by that date. Bowing to the inevitable, he extended the Club's tenancy to August

1 and then to September 1, by which time his patience (and probably that of his wife) was exhausted. He gave an ultimatum that the Club must leave by September 15, whether the new premises were ready or not: in effect, he evicted the Club. As a result, the Board had to hold its first meeting in the new clubhouse at noon of September 21, before the building was finished.

Grand Opening

As the grand opening of 800 Powell approached, the Board adopted the first house rule for the new clubhouse: that poker and games of chance would not be permitted except in the private card room. Then the great day came: the new building was opened on October 4, 1909. Curious members found a library nearly bereft of books, walls largely unadorned with pictures and some important matters like the daily room rates for overnight stays yet to be settled. The day after the opening the Board set them at $1.50 for a room without bath and $2.00 with and, probably reflecting a problem encountered on the Club's opening night, gave permission to the House Committee "to purchase about one dozen pairs of pajamas and one gross of toothbrushes for the use of the members who might have occasion unexpectedly to occupy a transient room...."

By general consent, the finest feature of the new building was the five stained glass windows on the third floor, commissioned to replace those of Bruce Porter at 722 Sutter.[16]

As a matter of history, the most interesting oriel is the central Club emblem because, to modern members used to the garlanded letters U and C, it is unfamiliar. The present Club wreath must have been adopted after the building of 800 Powell, although there is no record of when.[17] The third-floor stained glass is a modification of a design submitted by Bruce Porter in October of 1908, which seems to have been approved by the Board on December 1. But the Board had second thoughts; its Minutes of December 12 state:

After a great deal of discussion at various meetings, it was at this time resolved by the

Board that Mr Magee's crest showing the two letters 'UC' and lines emblematic of the setting sun enclosed in a circle, be adopted as the official crest for this purpose and the Secretary was instructed to have the necessary drawing made and furnished to the merchants to be sent to the manufacturers.

This description fits neither the central oriel in the dining room nor the modern Club insignia, and it must be assumed that what was installed in the new clubhouse was an interim compromise.

On October 15, at 6.30 pm, an official opening dinner was held, at which 750 tickets for the California-Stanford game were made available to members and guests. And to cap off the festivities, a ladies' reception was held on the afternoon of October 22 — the last opportunity women would have to see the inside of the clubhouse until 1942.

Early Years at 800 Powell

Settling into the new purpose-built premises was made easier by the generosity of members in filling the Club's needs. This was especially evident in the library. Initially, only $2,000 had been allocated for the purchase of books, leaving many shelves bare. But early on, Alfred Stillman lent 3,000 volumes and then William Stuart Duval, chairman of the Literature and Arts Committee, started an acquisition program to build a collection, so that by the time Stillman reclaimed his 3,000 volumes the Club owned a substantial number of books in its own right. When past-President Thomas Magee passed away on May 30, 1914 (he was found dead under his automobile in Sausalito) a memorial fund was set up to acquire Californiana, and George H. Whipple gave his fine book collection to the Club in 1917.[18]

A different kind of need - if need it was - was filled by those members who, over the years, have arranged for the Club to be the depository of stuffed animal heads. Yet, when the clubhouse first opened, none could be found: the earthquake and fire had put them in short supply. This became apparent to a group of members who wished to give one as a present to the Club.

The present-day emblem of the Club (shown here) was not adopted until after 800 Powell Street had been designed. In consequence, the central stained glass in the third-floor dining room shows an earlier version which was superseded before ever the clubhouse opened.

The 1909 Christmas dinner at the clubhouse was designed to stimulate giving. The format was described in March, 1945, by long-time member William A. Magee:

...the President and Board of Directors had decided that for the Christmas dinner there would be no tin horns or Santa Claus, but that each group of members who lunched together could be expected to present something which would help furnish the Club. For instance, that table over there gave an electric lamp; this one had given a set of books, someone else had given a framed engraving.

Magee habitually lunched with a group of sporting members, and the suggestion was made (which posterity might judge unwise) that they give a buffalo head or something of the kind. But Magee's group could not find among themselves an animal head to donate, so they collected $125 to purchase one. Even then, they could not find one on public sale and they finally bought an elk from the downtown fur store run by Sidney Liebes. At its presentation after Christmas dinner, Magee read a specially composed poem, "To an Elk's Head".[19]

1909's dearth of stuffed wildlife turned out to be untypical. Soon, they were being donated in abundance. On March 15, 1910, the Board noted that C.N. Black had contributed a "wild mounted swan", and on March 29, R.J. Davis donated a buffalo head. Over the years, additional trophies found their last resting place in the Club, remaining on the walls, slowly deteriorating, until relegated to the basement and then to the garbage. But even now, two survive to stare out unseeingly at the passing parade up and down the stairwell between the fourth and third floor.

Until the War

The years from 1909 to 1917 were good ones for the University Club; its members were riding a nationwide boom in which San Francisco was conspicuously sharing. Many were to look back upon the period's social events with nostalgia, among which the best remembered were election night dinners and the celebrations accompanying important varsity football games.

Before commercial radio had the ability to relay the news of the day across the country, the Club regularly arranged for a telegraph wire to be run into its premises on special occasions, so that members could hear election and football results at the earliest possible moment. Beginning in 1908, this was done on each national election night, when the Club always held a dinner.

Club historian Blaisdell remembered the presidential campaign of 1916 as particularly exciting around the Club, since Republican Charles Evans Hughes had resigned as a justice of the United States Supreme Court to challenge Democratic incumbent Woodrow Wilson. Across the country, "Hughes Clubs of College Men" were formed, including one in San Francisco. Many of its activities took place at the University Club: the Hughes Club was as dedicated to "much eating and drinking" as to

candidate Hughes: perhaps because of that, Wilson was re-elected.

These election night dinners, being held in the fall, provided an excellent opportunity to sell tickets for the California-Stanford "Big Game"; as many as 1,000 would be purchased at the Club during the course of an evening.[20] But the local game was not the only one to engage the interest of the membership. In 1916, inspired by the example of election night, some enterprising sons of the Ivy League arranged for a wire to be run into the Club so that the Harvard-Princeton, Yale-Princeton and Harvard-Yale games could be followed play-by-play. Members who were *alumni* of the three schools paid for this luxury.

Indeed, things were so good that the prewar period was one of comparative ease, even for the Club's governing body, except for a continuing rapid turnover in Club managers. According to the Board's Minutes, in May of 1912, one John Tait accepted the position and yet by May of 1913 it was held by R.R. Briare. Otherwise, the Board had fewer headaches than average. From time to time, the Board found it necessary to raise Club charges and prices, but not drastically. In September, 1910, it increased the Club initiation fee to $150 and in 1912 it raised the monthly room rates to a scale beginning at $32.50 and rising to $85.00 for a suite. Nightly rentals remained at between $1.50 and $2.00.

The Club's membership policy remained consistent, in particular in encouraging younger men to join. Although numbers were up even before World War I, they were swelled by those in the special category of army and navy officers rather than newly graduated college and university men.[21] In December 1915, an advisory committee to the Board was set up to devise means of recruiting new graduates and in June, 1916, the Board named Thomas H. Breeze as chairman of the membership committee with the special assignment of considering "what could be done to interest young graduates in the Club and bring the Club to the attention of students at the University of California and Stanford University". In addition, in May 1912, the Board asked Club members to approve a plan, modeled on existing arrangements for university instructors, by which foreign diplomats were permitted use of the Club without paying initiation fees and at half the usual monthly dues. The matter passed.

In fact, the Club already had a lively bunch of young members, who sometimes overstepped the bounds of propriety. The most serious incident occurred less than a year after the Club took possession of its new building. According to the Board Minutes, between May 30 and June 3 some miscreants committed "a series of boisterous and disorderly acts...consisting of destroying the Club property, throwing tables, bells, bottles and other things out of windows into the street and disturbing the peace and rest of other members...." The Board identified the culprits as four members and their three guests. Deeming this behavior "prejudicial to the interest and welfare of the Club", the Board fined each of the four responsible members[22] $250, payable immediately, and ordered that they be billed pro rata for the damage they had done to the Club's property. As to the guests, who were found to have grossly abused their privileges as visitors, the Board requested them "not to enter the premises again under any conditions, whether invited to do so by a member or not".[23] Not until September, 1915, more than five years later, did the members of this Board collectively ask their successors to forgive the visitors and "expunge" the incident from the record.[24]

The most important (and expensive) action taken by the Board in these prewar years was its exercise of the Club's option on the Turner lot, primarily to protect the Club's magnificent view of the city and bay.[25] Before the building of San Francisco's downtown skyscrapers, the clubhouse had a spectacular outlook over the bay, including Treasure Island and Mount Diablo: the campanile on the Berkeley campus of the University of California was clearly visible. So, in July, 1913, when the Club's five-year option on the property at $15,000 was about to expire, the Board notified Mrs Turner of its decision to buy. Financing was arranged by committing $1,500 of the Club's reserves and borrowing $12,000 from Hibernia Bank and another $1,500 from Crocker Bank.[26]

Hermes Joins the Club

An expenditure of a quite different kind was the purchase, in 1915, of the bronze half-scale statue entitled "Resting Hermes" (usually referred to simply as "Hermes") which is now displayed outdoors on California Street and has become a Club mascot. Originally, however, the statue was displayed inside the clubhouse.

The opportunity for Hermes' acquisition arose with the ending of the Panama Pacific International Exposition, San Francisco's world fair celebrating the completion of the Panama canal. As a part of the fair's Italian exhibit, Hermes had come to the attention of the Club's Literature and Arts Committee. In particular, Director L.M. Avenali advocated its purchase. The outbreak of war in Europe[27] had made the difficulties of shipping the piece back to Italy so great that the Italian government was even considering melting it down for scrap. It therefore appeared that it might be purchased for a price within the Club's budget; its art fund had reached $592 by December of 1915.[28]

Avenali negotiated with the Italian Commission to buy Hermes for $300 and by December 9, the Board directed Club Secretary Ralph L. Phelps to inform J. Chivarri and Company of Naples, creators of the piece, that the Club had bought it.[29] The statue was placed in the fourth floor rotunda of the clubhouse on an especially created pedestal of California travertine.

Another change in the interior of the Club was that the writing room[30] was transformed into a grill room. The successful campaign to do this was led by the future Club historian, Nathaniel Blaisdell and ingeniously financed by selling pewter steins, upon which a purchaser's name was engraved, for $120 each.[31] In 1918, Blaisdell was also in charge of a bedroom improvement project by which rooms facing east were widened so as to give each two windows and a separate bathroom, at the sacrifice of a room or two.[32]

Notes

1. Yet a communication to the membership dated March 1, 1905 regarding renewal of the lease of 722 Sutter Street said: "Under the new arrangement, as under the present lease, the Club will continue to pay taxes and insurance...." This would be a normal obligation of tenancy. Assuming the renewal was on such terms, the Club was either in breach of its lease or the insurance contemplated did not extend to earthquake losses.

2. The "double house" has been demolished to make way for an apartment building numbered 1817 California Street. Today, the address 1815 California Street no longer exists.
   Members of the Bohemian and Pacific Union Clubs were also welcomed to these premises.

3. Although the postal address of the present clubhouse is 800 Powell Street, it could equally well have become 880 California. The Powell Street address was chosen because the entrance of the clubhouse faces Powell: but had the clubhouse been designed deep from California instead of broad from Powell, the California Street address would have been appropriate.

4. According to the 1906 *Bluebook*, p.53, before the earthquake 1815 California was occupied by Mr & Mrs M.J. Brandenstein, Mr & Mrs F.W. Dohrman, Mr & Mrs F.W. Dohrman, Jr. and Miss Blanca W. Paulson, while Dr & Mrs Pischel occupied 1817 California, suggesting that the Pischels used half of the "double house" as income property while living in the other half. Possibly, the Club took not only all of 1815 California but also some of 1817, so that it intruded into space previously part of the Pischels' living quarters.
   The Pischels' pre-earthquake tenants relocated, but whether voluntarily or not is unknown. According to the 1907 San Francisco *Directory*, Mr & Mrs Brandenstein moved to 2210 Clay Street and "B. Paulson" to 66 22nd Street; and according to the 1907 *Bluebook*, the older Dohrmans had moved to Ross Valley, California, while the younger couple went to 1090 Page.

5. "Mr Thomas" was almost certainly Uncle Billy, founder of the Club and its first President.

6. They were:
   i. the northeast corner of Sacramento and Mason;
   ii. the northeast corner of Sutter and Jones;
   iii. the southwest corner of Sutter and Mason;
   iv. the southeast corner of Post and Leavenworth, known as the "little palace";
   v. the "Zimmerman property" on Sutter between Franklin and Van Ness;
   vi. Union Square, at the northwest corner of Powell and Post, and
   vii. the northeast corner of California and Powell.

7. But by 1909, the President was describing 800 Powell as "the best site in the city". *Annual Report* (1909), p.10.

8. Offers like that of Hopkins – of two top floors of a highrise – were to be heard by the Club from a later generation of developers in the 1950s: see chapter 8.

9. Although the Club's address has always been 800 Powell, the stables were referred to as being on California Street when first mentioned in the Board Minutes.

10. The dilemma of preliminary expenses arose from the unwillingness of the Stanford trustees to pay any part of the Club's feasibility study. By contrast, Hopkins, who was an entrepreneur, spent his own money in producing plans for a building on his site which incorporated two top floors for the Club.

11. The Club could add improvements as long as they did not bring the total cost above $150,000. In December 1909, the Club's total indebtedness for the clubhouse was agreed at $129,248 and the monthly rent for the first five years was set at $888.

12. The value of the land was fixed for the first five years at $40,000. Thereafter, the Club and the trustees would conduct joint appraisals.

13. The Hicks Company disappointed the Stanford trustees and the Club Board when, a little more than a month later, it confessed that it had made a $9,500 error in the addition of its bid, and the contract price had to be revised upward to $116,500. However, the Board noted on November 27 that the next lowest bid was $119,000.
   Clubs seem especially vulnerable to underestimates by contractors. When the Sutter Club of Sacramento built its new clubhouse, "almost immediately, overruns and unanticipated costs began to appear. They occurred throughout the project and with such frequency that they

became rather routine". Comstock 1989, p.119. *Accord*, with regard to the Vancouver Club, Reginald H. Roy, *The Vancouver Club First Century 1889-1989* (Vancouver, B.C.: The Vancouver Club, 1989), hereafter cited as Roy 1989, p.199, who comments that actual costs of repair and renovation of its clubhouse were higher than estimates "as usual" in the history of that club.

14. The Club wisely exercised the option within the first five years, in July 1913. The vagueness of the price term in the second five-year period would have caused difficulties had the Club procrastinated.

15. President Olney and Director W.N. Drown volunteered to approach W.H. Crocker for a loan, but – since an "athletic annex" was not built for another two decades – it may be surmised that satisfactory terms were not forthcoming.

16. Facing east, the intensity of their colors changes with the light and they have ever since been a source of delight to patrons of the main dining room. They depict the arms of leading institutions of higher education on each of the nation's major coasts: the University of California, Harvard, Stanford and Yale. By happy chance, these combine in a harmonious yet vivid color scheme.

17. An almost modern version decorated the front of the Club's *Annual Report* dated May 11, 1909, before the clubhouse opened, but presumably too late to change the design of the stained glass.
     A similar uncertainty as to origin exists with the Club motto: it is not known when *multarum filii matrum* was adopted. However, as the central oriel in the third floor dining room shows, it had been settled upon before the clubhouse opened; the motto is familiar even if the emblem is not.

18. Likewise, in 1931, James W. ("Billy") Byrne (President 1910-1912) left books and paintings to the Club, including one by Thad Welch of Mount Tamalpais.

19. Magee had promised that someone from his lunch table would make a speech presenting the gift, but no one wanted to do it in spite of there being "17 lawyers out of 25 at the table": hence the composition of the poem.

20. As noted on p.25 supra, ticket sales had been a feature of the clubhouse's opening dinner.

21. The membership lists of 1910 and 1916 indicate that the service category was by far the most numerous of the Club's special categories of membership and constituted between 15 and 20% of the total of members.

22. The members were Messrs C.R. Tobin, J.G. Anderton, J.E. Gallies and F. Thierist. Tobin was a member of the Hibernia Bank family.

23. This was harsh; the Club has very rarely declared anyone *persona non grata*. The problem has most commonly arisen when an ex-member or member no longer in good standing has continued to use the clubhouse as someone else's guest.

24. The guests were Messrs C. Payne, H.H. Scott, and W.P. Scott.

25. This lot was later to be the site of the Club's original squash court.

26. A year later, the Club borrowed more money from Stanford to pay for some repairs to the clubhouse foundation.

27. By the time the Exposition closed in 1915, Italy was a combatant in World War I on the Allied side and therefore its ships and goods were vulnerable to German attack.

28. The size of the Club's art fund indicates that in its early years it made a serious attempt to build an art collection. It is not known how large the Club's holdings became before everything – except for the Keith landscape – was lost in 1906.

29. There was a brief delay in taking possession because of U.S. customs, but this problem was resolved when Club President Charles H. Bentley had his own customs brokers take the matter up.

30. Designated a "periodicals room" in the original plans and located where the present game room is.

31. Unhappily, not one of these steins is known to survive.

32. In Bliss & Faville's original plans, drawn up when private bathrooms were an unusual luxury, in most cases a handbasin and shower was shared between two bedrooms.

CHAPTER 4

Prewar, War, Postwar

In 1914, most San Franciscans believed that the European conflict would be resolved quickly; the city's attention was focussed upon the opening of the Panama Pacific International Exposition the message of which was one of optimism and international co-operation. The war's only discernable effect on the Club was to push the prices of essential commodities higher. In February 1917, the Board had to raise the price of lunch to 65 cents and dinner to $1.25 — a harbinger of much greater financial stringency once the United States had entered the war.

A Faraway Fight

At its beginning, the war seemed far away and no part of America's business; day-to-day life on the west coast was scarcely affected at all. Most members felt detached from the fray. A rare exception was Baron J.H. von Schroder who, on August 13, 1914, just twelve days after Germany declared war on Russia, had his name placed on the "members abroad" list.[1]

Despite initial appearances, World War I eventually had a profound effect upon the Club. Before America's official involvement, some members were drawn away from San Francisco by war-related work, most notably Herbert C. Hoover, whose association with the Belgian Relief program won him national acclaim and started him on the

road to the Presidency of the United States.

Although the United States' position was one of neutrality, sentiment among Club members (and the population at large) veered more and more in favor of the Allies. The Club's own charitable relief work began when, acting upon a plea from Dr H.C. Moffitt at its meeting of December 16, 1915, the Board suggested that members should make a donation to alleviate the suffering of the people of Armenia. Within a few months, the Club itself contributed linens to the French relief effort.

As war approached, groups within the Club advocated preparedness. In early 1917, eleven members petitioned the Board asking that it call a special meeting of members "to endorse the action of the President of the United States in the present crisis and his cabinet and also to endorse compulsory military service".[2] In response, the Board actually called a meeting for February 17, 1917, but it failed to give the full five days' notice required by the by-laws and the assemblage never occurred; national and world events moved so rapidly in the interim that it was felt unnecessary to reschedule it.

Entering the Fray

Most members of the University Club supported America's entry into World War I and once the nation became a combatant, the Club and its members were extremely active in the war effort.

Entry into the war accelerated price rises and increased shortages. As early as July 24, 1917, the Directors found it necessary to halt the sale of gin, vermouth and Scotch by the bottle or in any bulk, and by October 2, 1917 the Board felt compelled to assess each member not in uniform $50.00 to keep the Club out of debt. The problem was not just war inflation, but the fact that many members had enlisted so that revenues from their patronage had greatly decreased. According to Nathaniel Blaisdell, eventually 60 members served in the armed forces during the 15 months in which the United States was a combatant.[3]

Huge recruitment drives were sponsored throughout the country. On June 4, 1917, San Francisco's chief of police requested that the Club's bar be closed on "Registration Day", June 5, from 7 am to 9 pm, presumably to ensure that no member would be distracted from enlisting by the Club's usual pleasures. The Board unanimously acceded to the request.

The Beginning of the Drought

Advocates of Prohibition used the war as an opportunity to link the issues of recruitment and the virtues of temperance, which caused changes inside the Club. On June 12, 1917, the Board ordered staff to comply with an Act of Congress passed on May 18, banning the sale of liquor to men in uniform. This statute, designed to encourage sobriety among military men, rather backfired; for months afterwards, enlistees were "stood" drinks by members. It was not difficult to find willing recipients of such hospitality. Some military men managed to drink more than ever under the war arrangement.

Uniformed drinking had anyway increased when, immediately after the declaration of war, the Club created a special army and navy category of membership with dues for members in the armed forces at $3.75 per month, substantially below ordinary dues. Then, on May 15, 1917, the Club began issuing "privilege cards" to officers of the United States navy and later to officers of all services.[4] These guests seemed rarely to subscribe to the temperance leanings of Congress: but the favorable state of affairs was too good to last. The untoward consequence of the legislation was recognized in San Francisco ordinance no. 4351 passed on January 15, 1918, which prohibited giving away drinks to armed services personnel in uniform.

Military recruitment also exacerbated the Club's continuing difficulty in stabilizing its management. The labor shortage caused by conscription, coupled with the Club's difficulty in matching the inflated wages offered by war industries, made holding and retaining men with decent managerial skills harder than ever. Although the Board's Minutes are sketchy for this period, they reveal that in May, 1917 a Mr Phillips was manager at $175 a month. What happened to Phillips is not recorded, but he was succeeded by William F. Roulo, who in turn resigned on November 20, 1917. By the end of 1918, Edgar Bergeman had the job.

In diverse ways, the Club supported the war. It bought savings certificates and thrift stamps and participated in programs to keep the morale of the fighting forces high. For example, in 1918, the Club agreed to assist San Francisco's War Camp Community Services in arranging an outing for men at the Presidio training camp on the Sunday afternoon of June 23. The Club requested each member who owned an automobile to take a man or men for a drive and then to dinner at the Club. Members without automobiles were asked to sponsor one of the dinners.

The Club's most ambitious — but unrealised — war project was to purchase a "University Club ambulance" for use overseas. It began on June 12, 1917, when the Board gave Donald Monteith permission "to canvas the members for subscriptions for this purpose".[5] Some money was raised but, unfortunately, the Club's effort fell short of the required minimum. On November 20, the Board debated whether to return the money to its individual donors, but determined on December 18 that it should be sent to other wartime causes if the contributors' consent could be obtained.[6]

Armistice and Peace: Normalcy

War had been a time of stringency for the Club, and news of the armistice in November 1918 was greeted with at least as much enthusiasm as had been the declaration of war. Nathaniel Blaisdell wrote that members welcomed back peace with "wide open arms and full open throat".

A year after the war's end, on November 11, 1919, the Club expressed its gratitude to those who served by honoring officers at a special recognition dinner.

With the end of the war, the Club, like the nation, made an effort to return to "normalcy".[7] In the first months of peace, the Board debated whether to purchase the small apartment building adjacent to the Club at 830 Powell Street for $22,500. It called a special membership meeting on May 27, 1919 to recommend its purchase, but the motion for purchase was tabled when the Board admitted that a $1.00 increase in dues would be necessary to finance the transaction. By this tabling an opportunity was lost which, many years later, the Club would regret; however, for the time being the matter was forgotten. In partial compensation for its disappointment regarding 830 Powell, the Board did succeed in gaining the members' approval for acquisition of the lot on the northeast corner of California Street and Miles Court. Up to $8,000 was allocated for this purchase, which was made and was to have great importance in the future.

All this was so reminiscent of the Board's prewar preoccupations that superficially there seemed to have been a return to business as usual. The reality was, however, that the postwar environment was a quite different one for the Club: conditions had been propitious for clubs before the war in a way that would never recur again. In the coming years, the Club would have to contend with Prohibition in the twenties followed by the Great Depression of the thirties, and then the tremendous hardships imposed by World War II.

Notes

1. The Board Minutes for April 1917 record that after the United States entered the war, "Baron von Schroder was expelled as being an alien enemy; and for nonpayment of his Club dues".

2. The eleven members were H. T. Summersgill, Allen I. Kittle, DuVal Moore, P. N. Wescott, William H. Hamilton, B. H. Dibblee, Harry N. Stetson, Guy Wilkinson, B. H. Pendleton, F. P. Cutting and Warren Olney, Jr..

3. Blaisdell believed that only one member of the Club, Charles J. Freeborn, had been killed in action (on April 19, 1918). However, the Board's Minutes reveal that another member, Henry Brewster Palmer, also died for his country. The Directors approved the following resolution:

Whereas, Henry Brewster Palmer, a member of the Club, has laid down his life on the battlefields of France in devotion to the cause of his country and its allies and of humanity;

Now, Therefore, Be It Resolved, that the Board of Directors of the University Club of San Francisco hereby records its profound regret for the death of our fellow member, Henry Brewster Palmer; that there hereby be extended on behalf of the Club to the members of his family sincere sympathy for their loss which is also ours; and that their sorrow is also ours; and that our sorrow is alleviated only by the knowledge of the nobility of cause for which he gave his life.

4. Anyway, from the Club's inception, army and navy officers on active service had been a privileged category of members who paid no admission fees. Original By-Laws, article XVII, s.2. This probably reflected the influence of the Club's First Vice-President, Frank Soule (U.S.M.A., class of 1866).

5. Ordinarily, solicitations for any purpose are prohibited within the Club.

THE UNIVERSITY CLUB OF SAN FRANCISCO CENTENNIAL HISTORY

6. Efforts such as this were common during World War I. For example, the Burlingame Country Club successfully managed such an endeavor.

7. A word coined by presidential candidate Warren G. Harding.

CHAPTER 5

Prohibition

While popular history remembers the "roaring" 1920's as a decade of fun, Club historian Nathaniel Blaisdell painted a different picture. According to him, the thirteen dry years were not really fun at all. Perceptively, he summed up the era by writing that the Club:

> bravely tried to hold up its spirits, but...outbursts of joy were rare and becoming rarer; Club meetings, Club dinners and Club celebrations became fewer and fewer until they nearly ceased....Distinguished visitors, if entertained at all, were cared for by particular groups or by single individuals....The Club could not sing the old songs. Its cheeriness, like its cheer, was synthetic.

Kennedy, the Club bartender, arranged a wake for the demon drink on Thursday, January 15, 1920, just before nationwide Prohibition went into effect. It was advertised by an invitation in blank verse of Kennedy's own composition:

> It may not be
> The proper thing
> To sit up with
> The Demon's corpse
> But believe you me
> It looks as if

He will be dead
A long, long time....

Kennedy had no way of knowing that the Demon would be resurrected within fifteen years.

At the Club's Christmas dinner in 1920, the first year of Prohibition, James W. Paramore and Latimer Callander sang a lighthearted song which poked fun at the new legal regime and the Club members who most noticeably ignored it. Sung to the melody of the then-popular "Mr Gallagher and Mr Sheeham", it was named "Mr Volstead and Mr Wright" after the respective sponsors of the national and state statutes banning alcohol. The tenor of the song, which had many verses, can be gauged from its opening:

> *Mr Wright:*   Oh Mr Volstead, oh Mr Volstead
> I've got a law just like that one of yours
> With a warrant I can search
> Anyone lit like a church
> And throw his liquor in the public sewers.
>
> *Mr Volstead:*   But Mr Wright, but Mr Wright
> Your law won't keep no one from getting tight
> There's been drinking here to-night
> And the tightest man in sight...
>
> *Mr Wright:*   Harry Simpkins, Mr Volstead?

Mr Volstead: Tracy Russell, Mr Wright.

It would be foolish to pretend that there was no drinking in the Club during Prohibition. As was said of another California club, "a salary for a bartender was paid every month during prohibition. It is a good bet that his duties were more than ceremonial and that the salary was well earned".[1] Indeed, Chauncey McKeever recorded how Hong, the fourth floor bartender in those years and a successor to Kennedy, ministered to members: "They'd get awfully drunk and he would make them supper. He'd make hangtown fries...oysters and eggs".

The Lockers

Such lyrics as Paramore and Callander sang no doubt provoked hilarity at the Christmas dinner, but they could not disguise the danger posed by Prohibition to Club life. Heretofore, the Club's hospitality had always been accompanied by alcoholic refreshment and without it things would not be the same. In recognition of this fact, as national prohibition went into effect, the Board approved, at its meeting of June 10, 1919, a system whereby members were permitted "to store liquors in the Club" and directed "that a locker system be installed for such members as may desire lockers, this procedure to be in effect as long as it may be legal". Actually, the legality of such locker systems was debatable from the start, but in the face of Prohibition many clubs across the nation instituted them. The theory was that since the Club itself was not dispensing alcohol but merely allowing its members to store their own liquor, it was not violating the eighteenth amendment or laws thereunder.[2] Blaisdell justified giving considerable details about the lockers because they were "of great interest to historians and anthropologists". He was right.[3]

According to I.F. Barreda Sherman, eventually each member came to own one of these lockers. They were originally placed on all the free walls of what Blaisdell called the "thirst room", which was the fourth floor bar, then located in its northwest corner (space now occupied by the directors' room and a men's room).[4] Churchill Peters recounted that the lockers were behind the bar and each man had a key to his own, so that a member "could keep his beverage[s] of any sort there, and enjoy them when he wanted to...." The bar was "a meet place for members who wanted to spend a congenial half-hour or so with their friends", Peters recalled, and "there were several who spent more than that time there and were well-known for doing so."

As the decade wore on and the laws became more stringent, the lockers moved around. After they were removed from the fourth floor bar, Blaisdell recorded, "for a period guzzling was done in a semiconcealed fashion in members' rooms, each member accumulating several roomers". Later, a few lockers were set up in room 14, known as the least desirable of the residential rooms. According to Blaisdell, this made "the poorest room in the house the most popular". After another lapse of time, some lockers were set up "on the top stair landing of the rear hall, next to the hall closet, then down the back stairs to a lower landing".

Besides its social implications, Prohibition had disastrous financial consequences; liquor sales had been a crucial source of revenue. A rule of Club economics, arrived at from years of experience, was that food service lost money while bar service made it.[5] Prohibition meant almost automatic financial difficulty for the Club, for which the locker rental fees were an insubstantial substitute.[6]

The Clubhouse Interior

What did the Club's interior look like in the twenties? Except for the lockers, I. F. Barreda Sherman remembered it as not greatly different from today: but although the general impression may have remained the same, many details have changed. For instance, then the Club's message tubes were still in use and not merely preserved as a historical oddity; a far greater proportion of floor space was given over to accommodations for members who made their homes in the Club; the fourth floor bar and several other rooms were located differently from today; and Hermes, instead of being as he is now, an outdoor exhibit, began the decade as the most conspicuous feature of the fourth floor, greeting members as they emerged from the elevator. But before long the fire

The north end of the fourth-floor dining-room, showing the fireplace and the Keith landscape above it. William Keith was a leader among western pastoral artists and an early member of the Club. This work, salvaged from 722 Sutter Street in 1906, has been in the same position at 800 Powell since its opening in 1909.

department insisted that Hermes be removed because his weight was too much for the floor to bear and he was ignominiously exiled to the trunk room in the basement, where members who lived at the Club left currently unwanted belongings. The statue was not to see the light of day again for many years.[7]

A Fine Gift

Among the happiest legacies of that era, making the Club look as it remains today, was a donation by the consul general of Chile, Marcus Huidobro, in December 1925, of a magnificent stained glass window in the style of the other university pieces in the main third floor dining room. It represented the coat of arms of the Real Universidad de San Felipe de Santiago de Chile, founded by King Philip the

Fifth of Spain in 1738. The glass was installed alongside the other university emblems. Huidobro, a beneficiary of the diplomatic category of membership created by the Board in 1912, made the gift in return for the courtesies shown him by the Club. The consul general's gift was fitting in that it augmented a feature of the clubhouse that had been valued since the Club's earliest days, going back to Bruce Porter's originals at 722 Sutter Street. A special dinner party to honor the gift and its donor was held in the Club on Christmas Day.

In spite of Blaisdell's rather bleak description of the atmosphere of the Club during Prohibition, it offered many activities in the 1920s. Then, the Club maintained a billiards room (where the fourth floor bar is now located) and also had, as it still does, a room for cards and dominoes.[8] In 1923, the Club succumbed to a raging national fad and purchased a *mah jong* set. The fourth floor bar managed to remain lively enough for many barroom ballads, some rather indelicate, to emanate from it. The leader of many songfests there between 1916-1928 was member E.G. Smedler. Some of the songs survive in a collection made by William H. Hutchinson in 1947, entitled *Songs of the University Club*. They are period pieces, capturing something of the atmosphere of the Club in bygone times. An example is one entitled "I Love the Girl Who Will":

> I love the girl who will
> Respect the girl who won't
> But I despise the girl who says she will
> And then she don't
> But of all girls that I adore
> And I'm sure you'll say I'm right
> Is the girl who says she shouldn't
> But who makes you feel she might.

What sort of men sang these songs and became members in the 1920s? Two fine representatives of that vintage are I.F. Barreda Sherman, who joined in March, 1920 and Churchill Peters, who joined in July, 1923: both had attended Yale (classes of 1915 and 1919 respectively) and upon returning to San Francisco from their eastern education were attracted by the Club's congenial social mix.[9] According to Sherman, the Club sought members who were "educated gentlemen. Somebody who would have a background somewhat similar to the rest of us, and who was likeable. That was the only requirement; that he be a gentleman, and was educated...." Sherman joined at the urging of his father, a long-time member, and Sherman *fils* was therefore already familiar with the Club from visits. He described it as a quiet, gracious and friendly Club, which he joined in preference to other possibilities such as the Bohemian Club partly because it had lower rates for younger men. But of all the pleasing things that drew him to the Club, Sherman was most attracted by "comradeship — having lunch with a good friend, or a group of friends, and having dinner with a group of friends".

Churchill Peters, speaking on a different occasion from Sherman, expressed his opinion that the Club in those days was markedly friendly:

> It struck me as being a very congenial group of people who were comfortably established and well representative of the city and philosophy of San Francisco. It seemed to me a very ideal group to be part of.

Mr Interlocutor, Sah!

At the beginning of the 1920s, the grandest event of the Club's calendar was, as it had been in the prewar years, the election night dinner. In 1924 the attraction of the telegraph wire run into the Club's premises for the election in which incumbent Calvin Coolidge would prevail was still great, but the improvement in commercial radio meant that election night beanfeasts were bound to be supplanted; and in 1926 the fabulous success of the first minstrel show, held in conjunction with the Club's Christmas dinner, showed what would supplant them. As the 1927 *Annual Report* observed:

> The minstrel show, given under the energetic and efficient direction of the Entertainment Committee, headed by Mr [Austin] Moore, and passed by the censor, apparently established itself as a Club institution, and deserved the enthusiastic support which it received from the membership.

From then until 1933, no social events at the Club were more popular than the annual minstrel shows. Indeed, they became so popular that the Club had to occupy two sites to execute them: dinner was served at the Club, and then members went across the street to the Fairmont Hotel for the show itself.

These performances showed that the Bohemian Club had no monopoly of Thespian talent. Over the years, the minstrel show became a showcase for the considerable musical and theatrical abilities of some University Club members, including the Paramore brothers, who made up most of the dialogue, and Loyall McLaren, who was always in the forefront as a performer.

The memoirs and recollections of several members allow a reconstruction of what these entertainments were like. Each show involved about fourteen players led by Loyall McLaren as the interlocutor, or master of ceremonies, in the center. All except McLaren wore blackface, regardless of what race they represented.[10]

The show had two parts. The first opened with a chorus sung softly before the curtain rose, but

The stained glass window depicting the arms of the Real Universidad de San Felipe de Santiago de Chile, presented to the Club in 1925 by Marcus Huidobro, consul-general of Chile.

Hermes in his garden. Originally part of the Italian exhibit at the Panama Pacific International Exposition,
this statue was acquired by the Club in 1915 for $300. Initially it was displayed inside the clubhouse on the fourth floor,
but it was put outside in 1965. The Club won a city beautification award for Hermes' garden.

increasing in volume as it lifted. Then, there were a few jokes between the interlocutor and two "end men". Such repartee was followed by more singing until the appearance of a blackfaced Santa Claus, after which the first part ended with the singing of "Jingle Balls", a ribald ballad penned by McLaren.

The second half of the show consisted largely of skits dealing with topical issues, famous people and current events. One poked fun at the "kidnaping" of evangelist Aimee Semple McPherson, later discovered to be hiding out with Kenneth Ormiston, a radio operator for her Evangelical Temple in Los Angeles. Kenneth Monteagle played Aimee, and James Paramore wrote lyrics on the subject to be sung to the tune of "Bye Bye Blackbird". Another skit was based upon the prosecution of the alleged rapist of vaudevillian Eunice Pringle, sung to "Let's Do It". Others humorously portrayed in the shows were actress Clara Bow and scientist Albert Einstein.[11] After such skits, the minstrel shows always closed with Loyall McLaren singing "Good Night Members" to the tune of "Good Night Sweetheart".

The Excesses of 1927

The tradition of the minstrel shows almost ended before it had begun. In anticipation of high spirits at the second minstrel show in 1927, the Club had deputed two members, Corry Janin and Churchill Peters, to attend the occasion costumed as policeman and keep order. Corry Janin was a husky man who had played on Harvard's football and baseball teams (and who had hit a home run against Yale and thus become a great sporting hero). Churchill Peters was a tall Yale oarsman with whom only a reckless man would pick a fight. Yet, in spite of this "police force", a regrettable series of incidents occurred which became the subject of a Board investigation.

At dinner, a guest from Paris was using a long cigarette holder. According to Churchill Peters, member George McNear confronted the Frenchman, bellowing, "We don't like showy things like that around here" and broke the cigarette holder in half. This "created quite an impression that things were

getting a little bit out of hand," observed Peters with some understatement. Nevertheless members and their guests went on to the Fairmont as planned.

Alas, misbehavior did not stop at the door of the Club. McNear, who had already created a bad impression at the dinner table, began, in Peters' words, to "get obstreperous down in one of the front rows". Peters and his fellow "policeman" Corry Janin:

...thought it was time that he be removed and we went down. While he was about our size, there were two of us and one of him. So we took him out, but that caused a little problem there. It interrupted the show....

Yet even this piece of summary law enforcement did not save the evening. Although the show resumed after McNear's ejection, worse was yet to come. The curtain, which was "a great big heavy sheet rolled up on a pole" hung from the ceiling, "was a temporary affair that somebody had rigged up...but they hadn't done it very securely". Somehow, its rope broke at one end and the pole fell and hit Richard McLaren, the interlocutor's brother, seated in the first row, on the head. "This really ended the show in no uncertain terms," recalled Peters ruefully.

Unsurprisingly, the Board was displeased with the turn of events. The minstrel show had been an official Club fixture; the Board itself had set the price of the affair at $3.50. It ordered a full investigation, calling in Austin Moore and Loyall McLaren of the Entertainment Committee to describe the incidents. Eventually, George McNear, A. Ropp and J.L. Thomas also made appearances, as well as the representatives of law and order, Corry Janin and Churchill Peters.[12]

The story of this night is not merely a insight into the Club; it also demonstrates the shortcomings of Prohibition, which arguably led, as it did in 1927, to greater excess than if social imbibing had remained legal. What Prohibition meant in practice was that guests, who could not openly drink during the dinner or the show afterwards, drank heavily beforehand in the hope that they could consume enough to keep

high throughout the evening. Churchill Peters observed: "Before any function of this sort, why, it was customary for people to partake in a little bit of stimulation, and there had been a considerable amount of that". He admitted that he and his fellow "policeman" Janin had also "partaken of a little". In such circumstances, breaches of etiquette were not surprising.

Ironically, the minstrel shows did not survive the passing of the twenty-first amendment. Although they were hardy annuals from 1927 to 1933, the 1933 edition was the last because, as Hutchinson recalls, "the repeal of Prohibition made the assemblage of a cast an impossibility". It was almost as if these performances were a desperate attempt to compensate for America's dryness: and in this sense, Nathaniel Blaisdell's judgment that the Club's cheeriness in the dry years was synthetic, was just.

ABOVE: *An undated newspaper cartoon by Swigert, entitled "Popular Misconceptions of Club Life in San Francisco – The University Club".*

RIGHT: *The original (November 3, 1847) grant of the land on which the clubhouse sits. Only fifteen months before, the United States had wrested this property from Mexico in the Mexican-American war. The Club acquired this document, now displayed in its library, in 1924 when it purchased two Miles Court lots from Mrs Sophia J. Flinn.*

The Business of the "Roaring" Twenties

The Club had other problems besides Prohibition in the 1920s; it was as necessary to take care of business in the twenties as in any other era. At the outset, postwar inflation caused operating costs,

TERRITORY OF CALIFORNIA---DISTRICT OF SAN FRANCISCO.
ORIGINAL GRANT OF TOWN LOT NO. *one hundred & twenty four*

WHEREAS,—By Authority of the late Government of the Department of California, power and authority was given to the Justice of San Francisco, to grant lots of land for building and improving the town of YERBA BUENA, in the district of San Francisco—as appears by the various orders of said government, issued at Monterey, on the twelfth day of November A. D. 1839, twenty third of April, 1841, and third of April, 1842; wherein the EXECUTIVE authority of the department, declares said power and authority vested in said Justice; and directs that the said Justice exercise the aforesaid powers. And whereas—those powers were exercised by the various successive Justices, until the 9th day of July A. D. 1846, when the district was taken by the arms of the U. S. of America; as an act of war between the U. S. of America and Mexico. And whereas—His Excellency ROBT. F. STOCKTON Governor and Commander-in-Chief of the Californias by his proclamation given at "Los Angeles" on the 17th day of August A. D. 1846, directs all civil officers "TO ADMINISTER THE LAWS ACCORDING TO THE FORMER USAGES OF THE TERRITORY."

Therefore, considering the above described powers, as shown by the archives of the Magistracy of San Francisco, as in full force, and binding upon me, having been duly appointed and qualified as Magistrate of said district; and considering and admitting the prayer of the petitioner hereunto attached; I *George Hyde* 1st Magistrate, and Justice of San Francisco, in conformity with the regulations, and usages, recorded in the archives of the magistracy aforesaid, do hereby grant, convey, and confirm unto the petitioner *Victor J. Fourgeaud* now resident in said town of Yerba Buena—district aforesaid—the lot of land lying and being in said town, containing an area of fifty Spanish varas square; said lot being numbered *one hundred and twenty four* on the present plan of YERBA BUENA on record in this office; giving unto the said *Victor J. Fourgeaud his* heirs and assigns legal, judicial and perpetual possession thereof, unto *him, the said Victor J. Fourgeaud his* heirs and assigns; for their own proper use, benefit and behoof forever, under the following conditions.

1st. The said *Victor J. Fourgeaud his* heirs or assigns shall within the term of one year from the date thereof have said lot, Number *one hundred & twenty four* fenced in, and a house built upon it.

2d. That said *Victor J. Fourgeaud his* heirs or assigns shall conform entirely, to the Police Regulations now established, or that may be established.

3d. That failing to comply with the first Article of these conditions, the said *Victor J. Fourgeaud his* heirs or assigns shall lose all right and title to said lot; and for the violation of Article 2d, shall incur the penalties which may be imposed according to law.

And that the said *Victor J. Fourgeaud his* heirs and assigns shall have a full and valid title to said lot Number *one hundred & twenty four* and be considered, and held in legitimate possession thereof; this Deed of Grant is given under my Hand and Seal, and recorded in the Archives of Land-Titles in the Magistracy of San Francisco, this *third* day of *November* A. D., 184 *7*.

George Hyde
1st Alcalde

Received, for this deed from the aforesaid Victor J. Fourgeaud Twelve Dollars and 50/100 the amount due the Municipal fund as per regulation duly established. Nov. 3d 1847.

Wm. Pettit
Municipal Clerk

This title to Lot No 124 is recorded in the Archives of Land Titles in San Francisco. Book B Page 32. & Fees for deed & recording $3.12½ & Nov. 3d 1847.

William Pettit
Municipal Clerk

To Joseph Mitchell
September 4th 1854.

including labor, to go up so much that by August 1923 a complete restructuring of the wages paid for kitchen help was necessary. The chef's salary was raised from $190 to $225 per month, the second cook's from $125 to $170, the third cook's from $90 to $100, and others received similar boosts. Inevitably, members were charged higher prices: and in November 1925, the Board even went so far as to institute a fifty cent a month rent for the lockers kept on the fourth floor.

The *leitmotif* of the coming-and-going of Club managers continued. On January 15, 1924, Edgar Bergeman resigned and D.D. Brachen was appointed to replace him at $250 per month, but by December 1925, William L. McCollum was manager.

At the annual meeting of 1922, the members voted the Board power to accept honorary members at its discretion. And in 1924, in a struggle which anticipated many later ones regarding the development of Nob Hill, the Board successfully opposed the Fairmont Hotel's plans to build a massive parking structure opposite the Club.

The Fairmont Hotel's plans for a parking lot reflected a change on Nob Hill; the area was no longer dominated by large private houses. It had got its name because the mansions of the rich had been there before the earthquake, but thereafter most of them were not rebuilt, or rebuilt elsewhere. Indeed, the fate of the site of Leland Stanford's mansion was to have an apartment house erected on it, which was later converted into a hotel; and by the 1920s, realtors were trying to sell vacant lots for institutional development. Coldwell, Cornwall & Banker's billboard at the site on which the Mark Hopkins Hotel was subsequently built actually suggested it was suitable for another club! From 1906 on, Nob Hill was destined to have more and more transient space.

In spite of the financial difficulties of the times, the Club took three immensely important steps to the Club's future during the decade: it bought several of the interior lots abutting Miles Court; it built its first squash courts; and negotiated the plan with the Stanford trustees by which the Club would ultimately become the owner of its premises, not merely a longterm tenant.

It had long been clear that the Club would benefit from having greater control over Miles Court and in 1923 and 1924 several interior lots were acquired in an effort to make it a Club enclave. Two of them were purchased for $12,500 from Mrs Sophia J. Flinn, who kindly presented the Club with the original land grant covering the clubhouse and the property immediately surrounding it. This document which, signed by Alcalde George Hyde on November 3, 1847, gave the 50 vara lot, #124 of Yerba Buena (the original name of San Francisco) to Victor J. Fourgeurd, is now one of the Club's prized possessions and is on display in its library.

The acquisition of adjacent property made erection of a squash court feasible. When the clubhouse was being built in 1909, some members had urged the creation of a squash court alongside, but without success. Nevertheless, the idea never really died: in 1910, a special committee of S.S. Lowery, Thomas Magee and H.N. Stetson continued to press the matter, and in December of 1915 the Board acknowledged that the addition of athletic facilities was desirable if the Club were to attract more younger members. But it was not until after the Miles Court acquisitions that the Club's first court was constructed, in 1929. In April of that year, the Board set playing fees of 50 cents per individual per half-hour and 25 cents a month for a locker. The facility, among the earliest on the west coast, was an immediate success; so much so, that by August the Board requested the Squash Committee to explore the desirability of constructing another, and by 1932, the Club had two.[13]

But the greatest achievement of the 1920s was to clear the way for the Club to become its own landlord. The Stanford trustees, from whom the Club's lot had been leased, had never been aggressive landlords and had more than once lent a sympathetic ear when the Club had temporary cashflow difficulties. The occasion of the negotiations was a reappraisal of the property due in 1924, which did not in fact take place until 1927. Over the next two years, an understanding was hammered out with the trustees, formalized by an agreement entered in February 1929, by which the Club borrowed

$169,000 at 5% per annum from them to purchase the clubhouse and pay off all bank loans and mortgages, on condition that the Club's debt would be discharged in ten years. But these arrangements were made in blissful ignorance that the Depression of the 1930s was imminent.

Notes

1. Comstock 1989, p.95.

2. By approving the lockers, the Board abrogated one of the earliest House Rules. Among those of 1903 (printed at the back of the *By-Laws*, pp. 57-62) was House Rule 3:

> No private wine lockers or private bottles of wine shall be maintained by the members of the Club.

3. As to the anthropology of lockers at the Vancouver Club, see Roy 1989, pp. 66-68.

4. This was the original floorplan of the Club, as designed by Bliss & Faville in 1908.

5. It was well expressed by the *Annual Report* of 1909: "The restaurant, as usual, has lost money, and the bar, as usual, has made money". Not very far into Prohibition, on August 30, 1921, the Board reported to members: "The Club is not on a substantial financial basis....You must... appreciate the effect of the 18th Amendment".

Other clubs have had a similar experience – for instance, it was asserted of Sacramento's Sutter Club that: "in sixty plus years, the dining room had never turned an annual profit". Comstock 1989, p.171.

6. However, they were worth having. Exhibit B2 of the 1927 *Annual Report* reveals that locker income from May 1, 1926 to April 30, 1927 was $609.10.

7. When, by 1925, various improvements to the clubhouse allowed Hermes to reappear on his fourth floor perch, President G. Stanleigh Arnold conducted a poll and found, according to the Board's Minutes of December 21, that "three quarters of the membership was against returning 'Hermes'...."

8. Not, however, the game room of today. It was a small room next to the billiard room. The old card room and billiard room were combined to make the present fourth floor bar in the 1940s.

9. Both men were to serve the Club as officers: Peters as President (1940-1942) and Sherman as Secretary-Treasurer from June 8, 1920 to July 11, 1922. Of his service, Sherman recalled that it allowed him to become familiar with the Club's operation and members quickly, and that he had the laborious duty of keeping the Board Minutes. As for his responsibilities as Treasurer, Sherman observed: "I signed the checks only after somebody who knew more about them had first signed them".

10. This was explained by James Paramore in *Songs of the University Club* (1947).

11. At a later date, the skits lampooned more political figures. After the election of Franklin Roosevelt in 1932, his "New Deal" was ridiculed. One piece, "Bankers Song", mocked the Senate Banking and Finance Committee for its investigation of bankers thought to be responsible for causing the Depression. In 1933, the Club used Ogden Nash's song "Quartet for Prosperous Love Children" as the vehicle of a lampoon of the national government's new policies and leadership. And later, F.D.R.'s controversial National Industrial Recovery Act became a major target.

12. Peters remembers that President A.R. Baldwin called him in on the following Tuesday to explain his conduct, telling him that the Board had considered imposing some type of restriction on Peters' membership, but then had thought better of it.

13. Apart from building the squash court, the Club spent only modest amounts on maintenance and improvements during the 1920s. In 1922, $10,000 was authorized for general "refitting and refurnishing". And in 1925, the Board approved a not-inconsiderable assessment of $50 per member to repair the third-floor balcony, replace the kitchen floor and various shower floors, to refurnish the back stairs and lay a new carpet at a total cost of about $16,000.

CHAPTER 6

Depression

The story of the 1930s had two major themes: the repeal of Prohibition and the persistence of the Depression. These two aspects of the decade were related; the Depression and drinking went hand-in-hand.

Prohibition was repealed in 1933, when Edward P. Haas was the Club's President. Once more, members could drink openly and an important source of Club revenues from liquor sales was restored.

The One-and-a-Halfs and the Repeal of Prohibition

Members took to the new regime with such enthusiasm that a new drink was invented, which remains a Club offering to this day. This was the "one-and-a-half", which is a martini with an ounce and a half of gin over ice, with a splash of vermouth and an olive or lemon twist.[1] The credit for this innovation belonged to a new young member, Chauncey McKeever. Alert to life's major problems, he had noted that the Club's 15 cent single martini was too small while the 30 cent double, served in a champagne glass, seemed to warm too quickly. He therefore introduced a new glass, with a capacity of about an ounce and a half, which the Club sold for 20 cents. Some economy-minded members, using eyedroppers and pipettes, conducted elaborate experiments, measuring out the single, double and the "one-and-a-half" to find out which had best value. Why this could not have been calculated as a simple piece of arithmetic is lost in the mists of time; perhaps it indicates a Club leaning towards empiricism. In any event, once it was proved that the "one-and-a-half" had more drink per cent, the Club had begun a tenacious tradition.

In due course, a "one-and-a-half" came to mean not only a drink, but a Club occasion. Once a month, a cocktail "hour" actually lasting one and a half hours was hosted by the Club at which drinks were on the house. Any member could participate, but it evolved into an adjunct to the Admissions Committee meetings at which prospective new members are introduced.

The relegalization of drinking confirmed San Francisco as "a drinking man's town" — which it had remained even under Prohibition. The Club reflected that: McKeever remembered that "the bar in the evening was fifty or sixty people pushing and shoving and getting and swallowing practically straight gin." This led to some wild evenings, the latter parts of which were spent off the Club premises. "I'm afraid some of the people used to move off in droves to some of the whorehouses in town," surmised McKeever. "Sally Stanford was supposed to have a charge account for the members of the University Club." Of course, the latter assertion is the sort of divine nonsense on which

45

Club folklore is founded: while it is just possible that some Club members adjourned to a brothel,[2] it is unlikely that an astute madam like Miss Stanford extended credit even to individual clients, let alone to a Club.

Retrospectively, the Club has found more humor in the age of Prohibition than it did at the time. To this day, in memory of dry times, the fourth floor bar displays two rare photographs of the "Carrie Nation Caper". The Caper was carried out by some Yale undergraduates who invited Carrie Nation, a leading advocate of Prohibition, to pose for photographs which were then doctored to show her drinking and smoking in the company of her hosts.

A New Generation Takes Over

The boisterousness of the Club's bar in the 1930s was largely attributable to a young contingent among the membership. McKeever said that there were so many young members in those days that the Club had to be careful about "people mistaking us for a fraternity house" - and with this appearance came some behavior "in more of a fraternity house manner than was agreeable".

There were other manifestations of this youthful *coterie* among the members. The squash courts — then new — attracted many younger men and according to John Lewis squash was the Club's most important activity (other than eating and drinking) of the decade. McKeever's use of the courts was typical:

I used to run up the hill from the Russ building, where I used to work, and by arrangement play two or three games of squash...it was always enough to get you hot and exhausted. Then you'd take a shower and get a glass of beer and a sandwich sent down to the squash court while you were dressing....

In addition, the Club fielded a rugby team, which played to small audiences in the stadiums of the University of California and Stanford. It was, recalled McKeever, "a very lonely experience with thirty people on the field and ten wives in the stands, worrying about the health of their husbands".

Alas, the influx of young members was accompanied by the demise of many old ones: the 1930s marked a farewell to many of the Club's founders, including "Uncle Billy" Thomas and Harold Wheeler, who both died between 1936-37. And a generation gap developed among members, reflected by the preference of some of the older ones for separate tables at lunch. Henry Hardy remembered that Nathaniel Blaisdell and James K. Moffitt and two others maintained a table, known to be theirs, and that, sadly, Cyril Tobin, the last of his circle of contemporaries, was to be seen sitting alone with a newspaper on a stand, eating his lunch.

But the older members were valued and in 1934, as a tribute to some of them, Thomas Hamilton Breeze's poems dedicated to and about the most venerable, were published for Erle Brownell by the Grabhorn Press — a publishing enterprise which was almost certainly Brownell's own invention — as *Round Table Sonnets*.

The "round table" referred to in the title was the informal but regular daily gathering in the fourth floor bar.[3] Expressed to be "in memory of Allen Kittle," a hundred copies of the *Sonnets* were produced. Each verse said a little about the man to whom it was dedicated, usually somewhat tongue-in-cheek. A flavor of the collection can be gathered from some key lines from the poems. For Brownell, the publisher (who was also a songster), "A lilting melody to while away noon's idle hour"; "but I fear you're too domesticated" for family man Perry Eyre; "In dress you reach the acme of perfection" for Henry Kiersted: and for dapper Henry Stetson, "Be lathered thou dost shave all thy four cheeks".

In this collection, there was only one poem that Breeze did not write: and that was dedicated to Breeze himself and written by W. Hamilton Lawrence:

Great Merit gathers at the Table Round
Hibernian seamanship, polo, the lure
Of razors, cookery and arts galore,
Chastity, gaming, wisdom, most profound.
But how shall all this excellence resound
In future ages when our noble corps
Shall be disbanded, and survive no more

Of those who saw us with the laurel crowd?
What would we know of Menelau's wrongs,
Of Helen's charms and Nestor's counsel sage,
Of all the craft and valor of that age,
Had Homer not embalmed them in his songs?

This final rhetorical question was apt; for just as memories of Menelau, Helen and Nestor would not have survived without Homer, what remains known of the regulars at the Club's round table of the 1930s is gleaned from Breeze's verses.

Some Depressing Aspects of the Depression

For all the lightheartedness of Breeze's poems, the underlying mood of the decade was gloom. When, in 1932, the Club asked Nathaniel Blaisdell, a member since 1901, to write the Club's history, he did his best to take a humorous approach, but he could not joke about the Depression. Ominously, Blaisdell's account of the Club in the Depression gave its dates as "1930 to 1932?" The question mark was significant. He did not know how many more years of hard times lay ahead, but was not optimistic that the Depression would soon end. He reflected:

To quote the most famous oracle of the Democracy: 'It is a condition and not a theory that confronts us.' The present Board has no theories to advance, no prophesies to make. Aided by an efficient management it is holding a steady course steering clear of debt and assessment, and appreciating the full confidence, patience and loyalty of the members.

This reassurance, although no doubt given in good faith, turned out not to be totally reliable: both debt and assessment were recurring themes of the thirties.

The ramifications of the stock market crash of October 1929 took some time to reach the west coast, but when they did they were nearly devastating to the Club. The crash affected the Club's members, as in turn the financial straits of the members affected the Club. By 1931 resignations from the Club became heavy: and that was only the beginning of a very lean decade. Reacting to the Club's increasingly precarious financial condition, the Board on May 24, 1932 cut all employees' wages by 10%, except those making $70 a month or less on fulltime. But it was not enough; another 10% cut was made on January 30, 1933: by this time, there was worry about the Club's ability to pay even its own operating expenses.

Routine maintenance of the clubhouse was suspended. John Lewis remembered that the bedrooms became "crummy" during those years, the bathrooms had "leaky plumbing" and the tiles were "loose and stained". The Board's Minutes do not record one major repair project (and only one improvement) during the entire decade, despite the generally recognized problem of deterioration.

The one improvement of the decade was vigorously contested: in 1935, a new bar and a pool room were created on the fourth floor at a cost — much begrudged by some members — of $6,075. Well aware of the opposition, on August 14, the Board, under President Edward F. Haas, decided to go ahead. Although the Board's reasoning is not recorded, it may be surmised: since the repeal of Prohibition, the Club's original bar had been found inadequate and the Board wished to maximize bar sales which had become the principal profit center of the Club.

This major rearrangement of Bliss & Faville's original floorplan brought the clubhouse into modern times, in that the fourth-floor bar has remained in its California-Powell corner ever since. Here, a member may gaze down at the busy intersection of the cable car lines as he sips a drink, viewing one of the few sights of San Francisco which has remained essentially unchanged since the clubhouse was built.

In the face of the Depression, the usual panacea for the Club's financial difficulties was tried: in January, the Board organized a membership drive. Director Gordon McIntosh led an impressive committee[4] in an effort to enlist new members and to retrieve recently resigned ones. In July, the committee requested that the Board lower the Club's reinstatement fees to encourage former members to rejoin. But this could not raise the Club from the economic slough into which it had sunk

Had it not been for the understanding of the Stanford trustees, the Club might have closed. By July 1933, the Club was having trouble in paying its mortgage debt and the Board decided that it had to seek some relief. President Haas met with the trustees and impressed them with the dire emergency with which the Club was faced; in response, they suspended the obligation to make further payments on the principal until January 1, 1935. But it is a measure of the Club's desperate plight that even this was not enough. Under the terms negotiated with the Stanford trustees, interest payments were still due and the Club could only make those and continue its day-to-day operations by borrowing $15,000 from the Crocker Bank in December. Before the Depression was over, it would be necessary for the Stanford trustees to come to the rescue of the Club again.

1933 was a bad year and 1934 was worse. The Club limped along from month to month, until all its economic woes concentrated in December. Little action was taken during most of the year, and when the Board acted, it acted on a relative triviality. On December 11, the Directors voted to discontinue valet service as a cost-saving measure — scarcely an economy of major proportions. The Board's pusillanimity in the face of crisis was the last straw for some impatient members, for two days later, a special meeting was called, at which twelve esteemed members insisted that the Board impose an assessment to stabilize the situation. They also asked that the initiation fee for the next twenty new members be reduced to $50.00, to both of which suggestions the Board acceded. But even these stratagems did not stop the Club's slippery slide in 1935, and some of the members who had forced the Board to assess the members in December 1934 were themselves leaving the Club by the following June because of their own financial problems.

Every sort of measure was attempted. The accounts of delinquent members were put into the hands of various collection agencies, and an attempt was made to collect from members and former members who had left the city without settling their accounts. And on July 9, the Board took the extreme step of authorizing the Ralph Crofts Collection

Agency to bring suit against a former member whose unpaid bills totaled $682.18.[5] The Board had, of course, always had the responsibility of pursuing the Club's debtors, but it had never resorted to such extreme measures before.

In 1936, things were not measurably better: according to Lewis P. Mansfield, the Club's membership dropped to an all-time low of 333 compared to its 606 complement of active members in 1924, the pre-Depression peak. In response to this state of affairs, the Board decided to waive initiation fees for the next hundred new members to encourage an infusion of new blood, while at the same time having to make the unpopular decision to raise membership dues once again.

For the first six years of the Depression, the Club — uncharacteristically — had retained the same manager, William L. McCollum, who had served in a position which had seen rapid turnover. Perhaps the ordeals culminating in 1936 were the reason that in August he resigned, having given the Club a total of a dozen years of service. He was replaced by Ralph P. Brennan, who took the job at $250 a month. It was a formidable task to undertake at this sorry stage in Club fortunes.

The economy's sick state was a constant preoccupation until World War II. Churchill Peters remembered that from 1936, when the Economic Roundtable of San Francisco was formed, to 1939, it met at the Club every Tuesday at 7 am for breakfast.[6]

A Little Light at the End of the Tunnel

As the decade came to a close, so did the worst of the nation's bad times. Even before America's entry into World War II, conflicts elsewhere had stimulated the national economy out of its doldrums, and after Pearl Harbor the country's productivity surged mightily. This had its beneficial effect upon the Club. In March of 1939, conditions had improved sufficiently for the Club to raise its nightly room rates to $3.00 for members and $3.50 for others. That same year, the Board resuscitated or initiated many reciprocal arrangements with other Clubs.[7] And by 1940, according to Mansfield, the membership had climbed back over the 400 mark. On September 18 of that year, the Board reinstituted admission fees for new members, which had been waived since 1936.

The Shambles

Reflecting the renewed spirit of optimism, in 1940 and 1941 an annual Club show was revived[8] under the name "Spring Shambles", as successor to the old minstrel shows. While the chorus was similar to the former presentations, it was done without blackface and (as its name implied) not at Christmas. Instead of an interlocutor, the master of ceremonies was called a "Shambolier" and was dressed as a satyr, complete with goatskin, horns, hoofs, and "smells". The show of 1940 was memorable for its rousing rendition of the Swedish "Helen Gar" and that of 1941 featured such songs as "Old Rebel Soldier" and "The Ship Titanic". Much of the singing was done by John G. Rogers.

And although the Club's membership count was far from ideal, new members were joining. Its facilities remained a major attraction: apart from the squash courts, the pool and billiard room (in the present directors' room) had a table that could be converted for either game and was quite popular. Henry Hardy, who joined in 1940, remembered being treated very well as a new man. He was told that some tables "were sacrosanct" for long-time cliques. He summarized the membership as "intelligent people of importance in and to San Francisco" and the Club as a place where the professions mixed. Hardy had lunch at the Club every working day (his office was at the bottom of the California Street hill): "it was all good conversation, usually about daily routine things, sometimes just pleasurable experiences".

But the Club's fortunes were not restored to total health. On the contrary, they were worsening: and it was not until the 1950s that the Club could be said to have returned to a healthy financial state. There is plenty of evidence that the decade of the 1940s, not the 1930s, most threatened the Club's survival.

The cumulative effect of the Depression was not fully felt until the 1940s. Churchill Peters, President between 1940 and 1942, recalled that at the start of his administration, "our cash position was so bad that we couldn't even get deliveries of supplies and groceries, except by paying cash on delivery at the door". By February, 1941, the Board had asked Peters to approach the Stanford trustees and the Crocker Bank to ask for a moratorium on payment of principal on the mortgage and, if possible, a reduction in the interest rate. But this was not easy and negotiations came to no resolution for eighteen months until, just as Peters' term was ending, relief was granted. Peters sent Frank P. Adams, a Board member, Stanford graduate and — as it turned out — Peters' successor, to talk with the Stanford trustees, and appealed to member James K. Moffitt, chairman of Crocker Bank, regarding the bank loan. As a result of this two-headed approach, on May 5, 1942, both institutions agreed to a two-year moratorium on the Club's interest obligation.

The Ladies' Annex That Never Was

An indirect consequence of the Club's financial plight was that women guests were permitted back in the clubhouse for the first time since its opening festivity in 1909. This came about because President Peters, casting about for means to improve the revenues of the Club's dining room and bar, noted that other clubs in Seattle, Portland and New York, with similar characteristics to San Francisco's University Club, permitted members to entertain ladies during certain hours and at specific functions. Although, as he knew "it was going to meet with great resistance", it occurred to him that the University Club might do the same. He therefore spent several months laying the groundwork, by finding out how "ladies' annexes" worked in Seattle and Portland.[9]

Since the evidence showed the financial results of opening to ladies to be favorable, President Peters and Frank Adams sent a detailed letter to all the members inviting them to attend a special luncheon meeting to discuss the subject. At this meeting, and in spite of some "old guard" opposition, Peters first obtained agreement that the Club should permit female guests, on the third floor only, after 5 pm. This proposal having passed, the meeting, in Peters' words "got a little enthusiastic"; it was then proposed

49

and accepted that the Club should investigate the feasibility of building its own "ladies' annex" by adding another floor to the building, accessed by a special women's entrance, equipped with an elevator, on California Street.[10]

This was an unforeseen turn of events at the meeting, and although Peters ascribed it to "enthusiasm", another explanation may be more realistic: once the original motion passed, the proposal for building a ladies' annex may have been put forward by opponents of the admission of women as a delaying tactic. Some support for this interpretation of events comes from Peters' own acknowledgement that many members did not want women entering the clubhouse through its front entrance on Powell Street: and the building proposal made it a precondition of having female guests that a separate entrance be constructed for them on California Street.

Whatever its motive, this grandiose proposition was treated seriously by the Board: there was immediate and thorough follow-up. Remarkably, in view of its fiscal predicament, the Club hired structural engineers to survey whether the clubhouse could withstand another story.[11] When an affirmative report was made, in the spring of 1941, architect Harvey Parke Clark was commissioned to prepare plans which were advanced sufficiently far by November for the Board to anticipate construction would begin on February 1, 1942. And so it might, but for the intervention of the war. Before construction could begin, a government agency ruled that no steel could be spared from the war effort for anything as frivolous as a ladies' annex to the Club.

But government preemption of scarce resources did not kill the entire idea and the decision to let women use the Club stood, even though, as Peters recollected, "it was very difficult to convince ourselves that it would be all right to have the ladies use the main entrance on Powell Street". So, on the night of April 23, 1942, the Club received its first women guests for more than thirty years at the first of many "open house evenings".

They were, in Peters' eyes, a success: he wrote on May 11, 1942 to fellow member James K. Moffitt:

I am delighted to say that the new program seems to be working out quite well. Mrs Peters and I have had dinner there twice already....Quite a number of other members have also taken advantage of the opening of the dining room and I have heard nothing but favorable comments.

He expounded on the same theme in a later address to the membership at large: "Not only has the response of the membership been very favorable, but these occasions have provided considerable additional revenues". Peters believed emphatically that the financial contribution was essential to the Club's survival: "I'm sure that it saved the Club from going into at least chapter 11,[12] if not further", he recalled, and his verdict was supported by others.[13]

Perhaps in response to the somewhat dowdy and neglected conditions they found, several of the members' ladies, including Mrs Peters and Mrs Lloyd Means, went to work in redecorating the third floor. Among the feminine decisions they made was to retire some of the animal heads from view which, said Peters, "met with approval of all except those members who had shot the beasts in the first place".

The Club's strapped financial condition meant that its staffing problems were acute: Churchill Peters explained that the Club's finances were so poor that "we couldn't pay decent salaries". While nationally wages were rising in response to war demand, salaries at the Club decreased; at the same February 20, 1941 meeting at which the Board asked Peters to negotiate debt relief from the Stanford trustees and the Crocker Bank, it decreed a six per cent salary reduction for every employee. This demoralizing situation caused the employees to be inefficient and dishonest including some, as the Club found to its cost, at the highest level.

In the spring of 1941, irregularities in the Club's books inspired the Treasurer to hire Price, Waterhouse and Company, certified public accountants, to make an investigation. Reporting on October 14, the auditors revealed that two "surprise examinations" of the Club's $1,000 petty cash fund had revealed shortages totaling $887, in circumstances strongly suggesting that the money had been taken by the Club's manager, Ralph Brennan.

Ralph Brennan had been manager since 1936, and with five years service in that position had been an incumbent longer than most of his predecessors. With reluctance, Peters and Adams confronted him with their suspicions regarding the petty cash, and he agreed to repay the money over a five year period. Neither Peters nor Adams wanted to impose any harsher sanction since, as Peters put it, "we were paying him hardly anything". This was not the last time that a Club manager would be found to have embezzled funds.

Of course, Brennan left his job: but this put the Club in a fix. It needed a capable manager, but could not pay enough to get one. A temporary solution was found by recruiting a young member of the Club, Mark Thomas, to take the position in exchange for

waiver of his monthly dues. Thomas was studying hotel management and wanted the position to gain experience in his chosen profession. He served briefly until enlisting in the navy just after Pearl Harbor.[14] After his departure, the same problem of filling his vacancy recurred. At the February 18, 1942 Board meeting, President Peters suggested that Thomas be replaced by John Maddocks, the Club's comptroller, who had shared responsibility with Thomas. The Board accepted Peters' suggestion, but recognizing that Maddocks would have his hands full supervising the day-to-day operations of the Club, decided to appoint member Lloyd B. Means as co-manager to supervise membership activities. As in Thomas's case, the Directors waived payment of dues in exchange for this work and in addition allowed Means a $25.00 per month credit against his Club bill.[15]

Notes

1. Today, vodka is sometimes substituted for gin, at a member's preference.

2. In her memoirs, Miss Stanford implied that the leading men's clubs of the city were a principal source of the clientele of her establishment at 1144 Pine. She mentioned most of them by name, including the University Club. However, since she did not set up business at that address until 1941, 1144 Pine would not be the establishment that Club members visited during the era recalled by Chauncey McKeever, if indeed they ever visited one of her establishments. Sally Stanford, *The Lady of the House* (1972), p.91.

3. To be distinguished from the Economic Round Table, a completely different organization, referred to later in this chapter.

4. George Sessions, E.H. Clark, Jr., H.V. Montgomery, Robert Montgomery, Richard McLaren, Charles Fay, Jr., Peter McBean, Allen Chickering, Jr., Roger Kent and G.H. Umbsen.

5. The procedure was that the Club assigned delinquent

accounts to collection agencies, but such assignments were not absolute: the Board imposed the condition that it must give permission before an agency brought suit. Hence, the Crofts agency needed Board approval before suing.

6. This was different from the round table in the fourth floor bar, which in general did not favor convening quite so early in the day.

7. This started in October, 1939 with granting of reciprocal privileges to the University Club of Tacoma, Washington. Over the next several months, there followed a spate of similar arrangements.

8. By members James Paramore, Lloyd Means, James Murphy, John M. Cates and John Holmes.

9. Both the University Club of New York and New York's Harvard Club were also experimenting with this idea at this time.

10. As mentioned in Chapter 3 supra, the Club could have been designed to face California Street and have an address of 880 California.

11. When the engineers were conducting their survey, they encountered, according to Churchill Peters, "a great many empty bottles of bourbon" on the roof. Peters theorized that they had been tossed there by a heavy-drinking member who lived next door to the Club.

12. A reorganization provision of the Bankruptcy Acts.

13. Historian Mansfield noted that this innovation "increased the usefulness of the Club to many" and I.F. Barreda Sherman said that it had suddenly become a "great pleasure" to go to the Club "for dinner before going to a movie or the theatre or whatever". And by 1943, by which time the Club allowed not only women but children of either sex as guests, the annual report, prepared by manager-member Lloyd Means, confirmed that "the opening of the dining room for family dinners and the establishment of a cocktail lounge on the third floor has worked out well. More and more members are finding it enjoyable to bring their family and friends to the Club". This positive response is remarkable when it is remembered that the clubhouse had been an exclusively male sanctuary for thirty years and that there were still a considerable number of permanent resident members, some of whom regarded the entire clubhouse as their territory. Of course, President Peters and Director Mansfield were "talking up" an idea that they had supported on the Board.

14. After the war, Thomas established the Mark Thomas Inn of Monterey.

15. Much of Means' responsibility would normally have fallen to the Club's Secretary, but A.M. Casey, who had held that position in early 1942, had enlisted in the navy.

CHAPTER 7

War Again

The Club did not do well out of the war: indeed, it lost sight of its own economic interest in its eagerness to help the nation in its time of need.

An Overgenerous Club

Many of the Club's members answered the call to military duty; the Club had a large number of young members. At the outset, it waived all dues from members in the armed services who were stationed outside the bay area, and allowed those who remained home to pay reduced rates. Naturally, this magnanimous policy is remembered by members who served, such as John Lewis who was in the navy, with gratitude: but it was extremely costly to a club already in financial difficulty. Before the war, the Club had some 250 dues-paying members, but by July 1942 only 169 remained.

Nevertheless, had the Club's *largesse* ended there, the problem might have been containable. But the Club went far beyond this, throwing open its doors to virtually any man in military service, either domestic or allied, without charging either an entry fee or dues. A serviceman had to be proposed as a special military member, but after that only a superficial looksee was given him before granting the privileges of the Club. And these temporary members had the privilege of bringing in their own guests! Small wonder that, as Lewis P. Mansfield said, the Club

became a "haven" for servicemen and that its annual report in 1943 made reference to the many military men who made the Club their "home away from home". Theoretically, they were responsible for paying for their own meals and drinks, but — as during World War I — uniformed men had trouble buying anything once they entered the Club's friendly confines. Peters was right to conclude that the Club "gave a great deal of pleasure and afforded the poor guys who were away from home and in the service some place to hang their hats in comfort".

A Fantastic Redeployment of Nob Hill

As early as the twenties, the Fairmont Hotel's plan for a large parking structure had sensitized the Club to the dangers inherent in the commercial development of Nob Hill. These dangers had abated in the 1930s largely because the Depression had halted development everywhere, but pressure returned in the forties, when an extraordinary new suggestion was put forward. It was proposed to turn the large patio of the Fairmont Hotel opposite the Club into a heliport.[1] Helicopters were then new and much in the news. The proposal so captured public attention that a local newspaper published a doctored photograph showing a helicopter landing on the Fairmont's lawn. Members had seen many things

Members have often seen pink elephants from the window of the fourth floor bar, but helicopters landing at the Fairmont Hotel may be a sign of a drinking problem. This "doctored" photograph envisioned a development which, thankfully, never came to pass.

from the window of the fourth-floor bar — but pink elephants had come before helicopters. Happily, the proposal was never implemented.

An Uncomfortable Presidency

In 1942, the Presidency passed from Churchill Peters to Frank Adams, who served until 1944. The latter inherited a bad position which became much worse;

after the first year of his Presidency only three of the original seven members of his Board were left, the others having departed to take on various wartime responsibilities. The number of regular dues-paying members continued to decline. Of the 169 there were when he took over, only 152 remained by mid-1943; and by March 1944, that number had declined to 128 — a number insufficient to sustain even the Club's operating costs, let alone service its debt. And the moratorium on the Stanford trustees' mortgage and the Crocker Bank's loan was rapidly running out: the Club's principal creditors were approaching, more menacing than ever.

In the face of impending crisis little was done, perhaps because there was little that could be done. On March 27, 1944, Adams requested members who

View from the Club's fourth-floor balcony, looking south across California Street towards the picturesque "gingerbread" gables of the San Francisco Residence Club. By use of the telescope at the far end of the balcony, members can see clear across to the east bay.

A comparison of this angle view with page 98's black and white photograph of Florence's palazzo Medici (now Riccardi), designed by Michelozzo di Bartolommeo, leaves little doubt where Bliss & Faville, the Club's architects, got their inspiration.

had belonged for five to ten years to make a voluntary contribution of $50, and those who had belonged for more than ten years to contribute $100. He explained that:

> those of us who are at home want to be responsible for carrying on the activities of the Club until our non-resident members in the Army and Navy can again return and resume their share of supporting and using the Club. We owe it to them and to ourselves to keep our fellowship alive until they can be with us again.

Adams explained the Club's need had been caused by "the increased costs of almost everything" and that besides the money owed to the Stanford trustees and the Crocker Bank, another $11,000 was owed for taxes and to merchants. "At a time like this", he conceded, "it is an arguable question whether or not the Club can function at all".

Many long-term members agreed, and as they wrote out their checks some of them doubted whether Adams' appeal was adequate to the Club's need. In addition, some felt that a factor not mentioned by Adams was at work: poor management.

As usual in the Club's history, there were problems in the manager's office, and under Adams a new manager, Henry C. Gordon, was hired. When past-President Peters responded to Adams' appeal on April 3, he commented that poor service, food preparation and short supplies of liquor at the bar were an "embarrassment to both members and guests". Furthermore, he noted that on a Saturday afternoon in the previous week, the Club had had no funds on hand to cash his check. But there was something else that rankled:

> on Saturday April 1st, [I found] that two [new] members whose names had been passed by the Admissions committee around March 6th, and for whom I was a second, had never been notified of their election to the Club and had become quite curious as to their status. These nominations were for regular membership in the highest paying dues bracket and I rather think were two of the very few such members

who have joined the Club within quite sometime. Notices were apparently sent out to the non-paying military members advising them of their election but income producing friends were neglected.

Thus, the Club's principal hope of salvation, the recruitment of new members, was itself being neglected. Peters' understandable irritation continued until the Presidency passed to Leon de Fremery in May, 1944.

De Fremery and the Crisis

Leon de Fremery's inheritance as President was a Club not only in deep trouble financially but one with acute problems with its hired help. In fact, an incident early in his Presidency convinced de Fremery that staffing was in more urgent need of attention than finances. Soon after he became President, he telephoned the Club office and asked for some information. He was met with the answer: "That's going to cause a little work. I'm not going to do that for a stop-gap President".

Although de Fremery knew that the war had made it difficult to find the right kind of employee, he was shocked at this inexcusable response. He thought it reflected poor management, not just poor help, and that unless the Club was managed efficiently its problems would not go away even if the fiscal position improved. The Club had had several managers in 1943-44; its usual experience with managers was exacerbated by the war. The current one was an ex-army officer with only a few months on the job, but his time was up; de Fremery fired him, for not arranging for "the proper help to represent the Club at the front office". On November 1, 1944, he was replaced by Edward Walsh, whose abilities immediately impressed de Fremery favorably: and, indeed, after a shaky start, Walsh turned out to be a most capable manager.[2]

Within weeks of Walsh's employment, de Fremery's attention was forced back to finances. In early December the Club received a registered letter from the Stanford trustees. It was not a Christmas card. It warned that foreclosure proceedings were about to be instituted against the clubhouse. A crisis had been reached; the Club faced losing its building.

De Fremery realised that he must present the trustees with a proposition which would persuade them to call the dogs off. He wanted to offer that the Club would begin to pay back its debt at $1,000 per month immediately, but great cost savings in the Club's operation would have to occur for that to be viable and to achieve them, he had to depend completely on Walsh. He asked Walsh if, were he to neglect repairs completely and cut corners in every other way, it could be done. Walsh said it would be difficult but, yes, it could be done.

Armed with Walsh's opinion, de Fremery met with the Stanford trustees. He outlined his proposition and then made a pitch to enlist the trustees' sympathy. He pointed out that the Club's current debt of $191,893 was too daunting. De Fremery told the trustees, "you have to provide the daylight", so that the membership felt there was really a chance of pulling the Club out of the straits. He therefore asked that the trustees cut the debt to $125,000 at once and that a portion of his proposed $1,000 per month payments should be devoted to paying off principal so that by December 31, 1947, the Club would owe only $102,727. Once such a positive track record had been established, de Fremery was confident that the Club would be able to keep up its payments and liquidate its entire debt.

The trustees were sympathetic, but added one condition to de Fremery's proposition: that the Club deposit $12,000 in a bank as, in effect, security for its performance of the promise to pay $1,000 a month. If within three years, the Club defaulted on that obligation, the trustees would be entitled to make up the shortage from the $12,000 fund. In view of the disappointments the trustees had suffered in the past, de Fremery thought that fair and he agreed to it. But where was the $12,000 going to come from? The Club did not have it.

The raising of this $12,000 showed de Fremery to be a shrewd tactician. Inevitably, an appeal to members was necessary, but he did not have time to raise the money in bits and pieces and concluded that he must approach a select few members who were

well enough off to be able to advance a substantial portion of the total — say, $1,000 each. Although de Fremery was going to ask for a loan, he conceded: "Anybody that could be expected to put up $1,000 would know that the chances of getting back his $1,000 were practically nil. And nobody wants to puts up $1,000 when he's never going to see it again". Still, de Fremery pressed ahead. He decided that he would invite eleven well-heeled Club loyalists, and eleven only, for lunch.

They came and I told them about my plan...to get rid of the debt and how the Stanford trustees wanted the fund. I said "I will contribute the first $1,000 to the fund". Well, of course they could see that left $11,000 and they could also see that there were eleven of them there, and that left no room at all for weaseling. They knew they were stuck and they put up the $1,000 each and the fund was created and the plan went into effect.

There was a touching aftermath to this lunch. James K. Moffitt approached de Fremery and said "if you had told me about this I would have contributed the entire amount". De Fremery replied, "I knew you would Mr Moffitt and that is why I did not tell you about it, because the deposit should not be a one-man proposition but more of a Club affair". This conversation showed not only Moffitt's dedication to his Club, but also de Fremery's astuteness. By demonstrating his fairness in not asking Moffitt alone to bear the burden, he had paved the way to a satisfactory compromise with Crocker Bank, the Club's other major creditor: for James K. Moffitt was its chairman. And although nothing was ever said directly about Moffitt's intervention, de Fremery was soon able to announce that the Crocker Bank had extended its moratorium on payments for the full three year probationary period during which the Club was paying $1,000 per month to the Stanford trustees and had indicated its willingness to take $8,900, the principal outstanding in 1945, in full settlement, waiving the interest it was owed. It was not inconceivable that James Moffitt might have played a part in this outcome.

The Club's Shabbiest Hour

The Club's "shabbiest hour" came about five years after Britain's darkest; even with its favorable new arrangements with the Stanford trustees, the Club was strapped and this meant, in de Fremery's words, that "then followed the worst period that [the] Club had ever been through". Every bit of maintenance that could be deferred to another time was postponed. De Fremery told Walsh at one time that if a chair had a tear in it: "Fix it up with a little Scotch tape".

There is plenty of testimony to the Club's shabbiness in those days. Some referred to the general state of things as "shabby gentility", others like Henry Hardy said the Club was "ratty", with holes in the cushions, ragged drapes and stains on the dining room walls from unattended leaks. Churchill Peters remembered that the place desperately needed painting and that "the carpets were all soiled". And Chauncey McKeever remembered the "moth-eaten and moldy" shooting trophies which had escaped the ladies' hunt in 1942 and still cluttered the walls. Their condition was so bad that, according to I.F. Barreda Sherman, the eye of an eland shot by Norman Livermore fell out one day and landed in John Renshaw's soup "to his great surprise".

Conditions like these made some members feel that there was no hope for the Club. De Fremery recalled that in the spring of 1945, Harry Magee invited him to a luncheon at the Pacific Union Club. When he got there, de Fremery found several of the University Club's oldest members present and the conversation made de Fremery realise that "they thought the Club was going out of existence and they were there to give it a decent burial." After the last eulogy, Magee asked de Fremery if he would like to say something. What he said was far from *requiescat in pace.*

> I said I was sorry that I had not been told the purpose of the meeting because if I had I certainly would have explained that the Club was decidedly not going out of business. In fact, I said I had just concluded an agreement with the Stanford trustees and outlined to them

what that agreement was. Accordingly, we made a rather lame attempt to transform what amounted to a wake into some kind of renewal celebration.

The Free Dinner

De Fremery's financial manipulations soon showed results. By March 10, 1945, he was able to write to members that all merchants' accounts were current and that in the preceding three months the Club had been profitable. But he did not wish to encourage complacency and urged members to make their own contributions: "we cannot expect our creditors to be the only contributors to the financial improvements of the Club". But morale among the general body of members remained low and fundraising was not a high priority for men preoccupied by the war. Evidence of this had been provided at the annual meeting of 1944, when de Fremery had been elected to office: only three members had been present, far short of a quorum. This was unhealthy and de Fremery was determined to change it by giving members an incentive to attend. He told Walsh, the manager, "I'm not going to have such a thing in my administration; so what I'm going to do is when I send out notices of the annual meeting, I'm going to say that at the conclusion of the meeting dinner will be served to all the members present for which there will be no charge."

Walsh, who had been given the great challenge of righting the Club's financial woes, protested to "Mr D" (as he always called de Fremery) that this would add to the Club's deficit. De Fremery thought otherwise. He pointed out that the service and facility overhead for dinner was fixed and that the only variable was the food, which was comparatively inexpensive. He predicted that profits from bar sales would easily cover the cost of a free dinner. The event proved de Fremery right; the annual meeting of 1945 was well attended and made money for the Club despite the free dinner. In this innovation, de Fremery began a Club tradition which survives to this day and, as it turned out, he had ensured that the membership would face peace on a full stomach.

Notes

1. The term "heliport" had not yet been coined; the proposal spoke of "a vertical landing field".

2. Shortly after Walsh was hired, de Fremery discovered that he had temporarily financed his gambling to the tune of $3,000 by asking one of the Club's principal suppliers to defer cashing a Club check for that amount. Instead of firing him, de Fremery said that he would keep Walsh on if he would promise that "as long as you're manager of the Club, you will never again play the races". Walsh agreed, was as good as his word, and thereafter was devoted to de Fremery and the Club.

CHAPTER 8

Peace and Prosperity

Peace was almost as eventful as war in San Francisco. The city was host to the founders of the United Nations and many delegates frequented the Club: Cyrus Eaton, a member of the United States delegation, used it to hold meetings and Lord Halifax, the British ambassador, often lunched at the Club. Of the latter, Henry Hardy recalled, "He had a table he liked. No one bothered him and, unless invited, no one would go over and engage him in conversation". Those invited repeatedly apologized for the appearance of the clubhouse, still unrestored from the war. Halifax usually responded by saying he felt at home in the rundown surroundings, since they reminded him of the clubs in London.

Renaissance

United Nations delegates were not the only ones who converged on the Club when the war was over; members who had served in the military came back to swell the Club's revenues. The Club's calendar reverted to a semblance of peacetime's joys, including such occasions as "epicure night". Conditions were good enough by the spring of 1946 for de Fremery to push for and get a dues increase and then an increase to the Club's initiation fee. As a result, the Club had, for the first time in over twenty years, a surplus to spend on long-delayed repairs.

The expected course of events was that de Fremery would step down from the Presidency after serving a two year term. But, according to him, "the men who had advanced the money for the deposit [imposed as a condition of the arrangement with the Stanford trustees] insisted that I serve for another year, which would see the completion of the Stanford agreement...." So it was that de Fremery served a third year in office and saw the Stanford trustees release the $12,000 and the Club repay all those who had stumped up $1,000 with 12% interest. When de Fremery handed over the Presidency to S. Vilas Beckwith, Jr. in May of 1947, he had the satisfaction of knowing that he had saved the Club from dissolution in its worst crisis.

In the immediate postwar years, there were many signs of a renaissance in the Club. For one thing, Henry Hayes, Bourne Hayne and William Hutchinson revived the Club show, the "Shambles", for two last years in 1946 and 1947. Manpower was still at a premium and so there was no chorus as there had been before the war. Instead the Shambles consisted of a musical with a smaller cast dealing with current affairs and various goings-on at and around the Club. The show of 1946 featured the song "North Side of Jackson Street" by William Hutchinson and the ribald "Cats on Housetops", while in 1947, Hutchinson provided two more songs, entitled respectively "The Miner's Heir" and "The Girl".

SONGS
OF THE UNIVERSITY CLUB

✦✦ EDITED BY WILLIAM H. HUTCHINSON FROM
MATERIAL LARGELY FURNISHED BY JAMES W.
PARAMORE ✦✦ HISTORICAL DATA THROUGH
THE COURTESY OF NATHANIEL BLAISDELL ✦✦
PRIVATELY PRINTED FOR FRANK P. ADAMS IN
THE INTERESTS OF THE CLUB & THE EDIFICATION
OF THE MEMBERS ✦✦ SAN FRANCISCO ✦✦ 1947

The frontispiece of Songs of the University Club *(1947), of which 400 copies were privately printed. The silhouetted figures represent "Shamboliers" – the presiding characters of the Club's annual show, the "Shambles".*

Notwithstanding that the Shambles was recognized to be funny, 1947 was its last year. It appealed only to one segment of the membership; tastes had changed since before the war. Some members, such as Chauncey McKeever, thought it was "too collegiate" and "just a...vulgar, rowdy, dirty show". No such enterprise has been mounted in the Club since then.

In commemoration of the talents displayed in these Club shows, in 1947, William Hutchinson edited *Songs of the University Club*, with contributions from James W. Paramore, which was

dedicated to past-President Frank Adams. It was privately printed in a handsome edition of 400 copies and featured many of the songs from the minstrel shows and the Shambles.

A new generation of members was taking over. By 1949, when Theodore Eliot joined, heavier use was being made of the clubhouse than had been seen for years. Eliot explained this by pointing out that many of the members who had returned from the war and lived in the city found the Club a convenient and congenial rendezvous in the afternoon and evening. But Eliot's explanation is as interesting for what it did not say as what it said: a consequence of the war was that the number of resident members, once the mainstay of the Club, had dwindled. They were no longer the dominant force. Their decline in numbers was to have important consequences fiscally and for the Club's ambiance.

In the meantime, the Club seemed to be enjoying a streak of good luck. One day in 1947, Henry Hardy, then chairman of the House Committee, was looking for a broom in the library in order to do a little housework himself when he discovered in one of the many compartments built into the library shelves two original volumes of Audubon prints. All except six of these were sold for a handsome amount, and four now adorn the walls of the third-floor dining room.[1]

Riding High

In startling contrast with the lean years of the thirties and forties, the Club had its most prosperous decade ever in the fifties. Its new-found affluence had many manifestations. The Club was able to afford such extensive improvements that member Mansfield, who updated Blaisdell's history of the Club in 1954, referred to the decade as "the spick and span" period; the Stanford loan was further reduced and an apartment building on Joice Street (to the east of the clubhouse) was purchased.

Expenditures on the clubhouse were long overdue. Years of neglect meant that nearly every aspect of its fabric needed attention; indeed, the premises were becoming reminiscent of an underfunded fraternity house. A program of upgrading was initiated, aided by three assessments imposed upon members between 1948 and 1954. In 1947-1949, the elevator and kitchen were overhauled; in 1949-51 the third floor dining room was upgraded; in 1951-53, the entire building was painted and, with the help of more than $2,500 in voluntary contributions from members, the fourth floor lounge was redecorated. In 1953-1954 and again in 1958, the Cable Car room was refurbished. During the next Presidency, new carpeting was installed in the library and — a sign of the times — the Club purchased its first television set for $500. The Club was doing so well in 1954 that the Board was able to set aside $17,000 to spend on repairing the plumbing and further clubhouse remodeling. On April 21, 1959 the Board approved a long-range plan for improvement of the lobby, the third floor and (once again) the elevator costing $50,000,[2] to fund which a $50 assessment was made on each member and two loans from the Crocker Bank were taken out, one of $34,000 and a later one for $2,000.

Some members liked the Club's shabbiness and mourned its passing: at the 1952 annual meeting, Bourne Hayne remarked (perhaps not totally seriously) that "the charm of the Club is lost when it changes to a State of Sound Finances". But what some would call charm others called squalor; and the membership's enthusiasm for improvement was evidenced by its voluntary contributions made to speed the process.

An improvement of 1952 deserves special mention. Ever since the Club had been at 722 Sutter, it had had some stained glass windows; the specifications of the 800 Powell building had included new stained glass renditions of the insignia of the University of California, Harvard, Stanford and Yale for the windows of the third-floor dining room. But as the Chilean consul-general had recognized in 1925 by his generous gift of a window honoring the University of Santiago, there was space for more. Perhaps inspired by his example (although much removed in time from it), members from seven additional universities donated windows commemorating their respective colleges and universities at a dedicatory dinner held on January 27, 1953, presided over by James K. Moffitt.[3]

Another sort of improvement, of the boot kind in

that it cost the Club nothing, was the transformation of a dimly lit T-shaped hallway on the fourth floor, which some members called "the black hole of Calcutta", into a small art gallery. Member Henry Hardy approached the Literature and Arts Committee to ask that he might hang some of his own work there, replacing "a very dark painting by Rollo Peters which could not be seen even in a good light".[4] The Committee welcomed this suggestion. In the years to come, other member-artists exhibited on the fourth floor and then later guest artists did so by invitation. The opportunity to exhibit at the University Club has come to have considerable prestige in the artistic community, and some guest artists have designed handsome posters for their shows.[5]

Debt Reduction and an Acquisition

The Club was doing well. By 1954, it had reduced its debt to the Stanford trustees to $79,600 and at its April 15 meeting the Board moved to pay an extra $1,000 towards it "in view of favorable financial results for the past year". The same thing was done in April of 1955 and in February 1956 the Board approved payment of another $5,000 on the loan. In March, 1957, the Board paid a further $3,000 toward it. These additional payments towards the principal of the Stanford loan were a barometer of the Club's new-found financial health.

In 1956 the Board appointed President Richard Ernst and past-President Harry E. Miller, Jr. to negotiate the renewal of the loan with the Stanford trustees and by December a favorable agreement had been concluded. The Club was to pay installments of $700 a month and had the right to make incremental payments in multiples of $100 at its discretion. The new interest rate was set at 4 1/2%. At this stage, only $59,384 remained to be repaid.

While the Club's indebtedness on its clubhouse was being reduced, its finances were strong enough to acquire a property to its east for the purpose of preserving its view, an action strongly reminiscent of that taken in 1913 when the Turner lot was bought. Although downtown skyscrapers had already begun to obstruct the Club's panorama, it was still spectacular. So when, in 1952, the Board learned that

Figure Drawing 12" x 16" 1986

CATHERINE COLCORD
University Club Art Gallery, San Francisco

Dec. 1-Dec. 31 ● Painting, Drawing, Photography, Sculpture, Graphic Art, Poster Art, Silk-Screened, & Mixed Media Prints

Catherine Colcord ©1986

ABOVE: *The View that was Lost. Downtown from the Club, c.1954. The Club's battle to retain this easterly view was finally lost in 1982, when the city started building the Geen Mun Neighborhood Center on the corner of Sacramento and Stockton.*

LEFT: *A poster advertising one of the many art exhibits which have been held in the Club's gallery. Since its foundation in the 1950s, the gallery has become well-known in the artistic community as an excellent place to hold a showing.*

a developer was acquiring land between Joice Street and the clubhouse for the purpose of constructing a highrise, it decided to try to block him by buying a small apartment house at 123 Joice Street,[6] smack in the middle of the planned development. On December 3, 1952, the Board authorized President J.A. Ducournau to investigate its acquisition and on December 10 further authorized borrowing of $21,000 from member William H. Grace and his wife Ann for this purpose.[7] The apartment building was bought in April, 1953, a rental agency was retained to manage the building on the Club's behalf and — for a time — the Club's view had been saved.

Small wonder that the atmosphere of the 1953 annual meeting was decidedly upbeat; Acting Secretary Richard Ernst reported that the 56 members present were called to order only after "considerable delay due to extended patronage of the bar and much good roast beef". At the meeting, Clay Miller rose and "commented on the rejuvenation of the Club, the refurnishing of the clubhouse, the high standard of the Club's spirit; he then moved a rousing vote of thanks to retiring President Ducournau, for his splendid accomplishments and contributions to

NEW HOTEL—This is an artist's drawing of the proposed 23 floor luxury hotel at Powell and California. It would be built on the present site of the University Club which would have quarters in the structure.

Fortune Finder's Wife Irks Judge

The wife of a Fresno man who found $350,000 worth of cash and stocks in an old stove was accused of evasiveness yesterday when she testified in court that she had never seen the fortune or discussed it with her husband.

The accusation came from Superior Judge Harry J. Neubarth, who was further irritated by the fact that the husband, Carl 36, a disabled war veteran and furniture dealer, did not show up for the hearing.

Appearing as the only witness, Mrs. Marguerite Scott, a portly schoolteacher, said that each time her husband brought up the treasure "I would tell him to keep quiet.

"The whole thing is horrid. Honestly, judge, believe me," she added.

Scott found the fortune in a stove he bought at a Bank of America auction last fall. The bank is guardian for Walter Stephen Brooks, 80, a Mission District recluse, who owned the securities and cash. Brooks was declared mentally incompetent and is now in a Sonoma rest home.

Judge Neubarth told Scott's attorney, Don C. Mayes, of Merced, that he considered Mrs. Scott's testimony "evasive."

"I can't imagine that a wife wouldn't discuss this with her husband or even be curious enough to look at the securities and bills," the court said.

Neubarth also chided Mayes for not bringing Scott in.

Attorneys for both sides finally agreed that Scott and his wife will both appear before Neubarth next Wednesday at 11 a.m.

"It's The Examiner for Want Ads"—9 out of 10 say it!

Plans for 23-Story Nob Hill Hotel Told

Details of plans for a 23 floor luxury hotel on the Bay-side slope of Nob Hill were disclosed here yesterday.

The new building, with 600 rooms, and interior garage facilities for 600 automobiles, would be erected at the northeast corner of California and Powell Sts. on a site now occupied by the four story University Club.

Cost of construction of the slender 'T' shaped hotel is $8,000,000.

The proposed operator-lessee of the hotel is Joseph Massaglia Jr., owner of a chain of hotels including the Sainte Claire in San Jose, the New Yorker in Manhattan and the Waikiki Biltmore in Hawaii.

SITE PARLEY.

Negotiations for the site are expected to be concluded soon between the University Club and Joseph R. Moser of J. E. Moser and Associates and W. Gustave von Loewenfeldt of Umbsen, Kerner and Stevens.

Terms call for a long term lease on the property from the club with provision that it will have the 21st and 22nd floors of the hotel for occupancy.

Officials of the two real estate interests involved in the transaction said it would take from 18 months to two years to erect the building after completion of the lease agreements.

The University Club would have a private entrance on Powell St. and elevator to its quarters on the upper floors.

MAIN ENTRANCE.

The main entrance of the hotel building would be Powell St. The main floor of the structure would house the hotel lobby, administrative offices, service shops and stores and dining room facilities.

A mezzanine floor would provide main kitchen facilities, lounges and private dining rooms. The second floor also would have dining rooms and convention and meeting rooms.

The top floor of the hotel would be a sky lounge with a restaurant, bar, dining room and meeting rooms. It will have an unobstructed view of downtown San Francisco, the Bay and Marin County and the East Bay.

FACING BAY.

The "Tee" shape of the hotel will be such that the top of the "T" will face the Bay. The base portion will be parallel to California St. extending from Powell St. down the slope to Joice St.

The parking facilities will be in two sub-basements of the structure. The financial backers of the project were not identified, but Loewenfeldt and Moser said adequate financing has been assured.

The thing the proposed hotel would accomplish would be to place an effective screen of the Bay view to some guests at the Fairmont Hotel. Owner Ben Swig took the announcement of competition graciously, however. He said:

"What can you do? You can't stop progress in this city.

"When you buy a piece of property you always take the chance that some one will build a bigger building in front of you.

"Besides, it's a very big Bay and maybe we'll go higher," he laughed.

Philip S. Ehrlich, attorney in San Francisco for hotel man Conrad Hilton, said the proposed new hotel on Nob Hill probably would not affect Hilton's plans for one in the block bounded by O'Farrell, Ellis, Mason and Taylor Sts.

Hilton's plans for the 1,000 room $20,000,000 structure are progressing nicely, Ehrlich said.

[the] results described. The entire membership joined in this vote". Ducournau's encomium was well-deserved, but members' pleasure in the acquisition of 123 Joice Street was to be short-lived. Not only did ownership of the building fail to ensure that the view would be preserved, but the Club was to suffer problems with its tenants while making only a poor return as its landlord.

The Developers Cometh

President Ducournau had acted in the face of a widespread postwar interest in developing Nob Hill, in which the Club had consistently refused to participate. Its rebuffing of the blandishments of developers since then reflects a pattern begun by the Board of 1952. The decade was one characterized by persistent attempts to develop all around the clubhouse and, indeed, to purchase the clubhouse itself.

The first inquiry, made in 1952, was startlingly reminiscent of the Hopkins proposal made to the Club in 1907.[8] The proposition was put that a 20 story hotel should be erected on the Club site and the Club be given the top two stories, accessed by a private Club entrance and elevator. The proposal would preserve the Club's view and guarantee its future maintenance; but the Board rejected it on the ground that the Club would lose control over its affairs.[9] It was against this background that 123 Joice Street had been acquired.

However, developers do not succeed by being shrinking violets and over the eighteen months beginning in May 1956 would-be developers made headway; a special committee, consisting of past-Presidents Ducournau and Dakin, plus member Fred H. Merrill, was appointed to investigate a proposal and the annual meeting of 1957 was dominated by the topic. Deliberations continued for many months and in October 1957, the Board outlined its requirements: the Club would receive at least 20,000

This press clipping from the early 1950s reflects the optimism of one of a succession of developers who have wished to exploit the Club's site.

square feet on an upper floor of the proposed building plus athletic and storage areas. However, by January 1958 the Board voted to disband the special committee without further action being taken, unless otherwise instructed by the membership; sentiment was against it and the matter was dropped.

Even this was not the end of the Club's courtship. In 1959, a Los Angeles developer invited President Theodore L. Eliot and Treasurer Robert E. Henderson to a "fancy, fancy lunch" at the Palace Hotel. Again, the proposal was to build a highrise hotel in which the Club would have space. Eliot asked: "Well, can the Club have the two top floors?" The answer was "no", the Club would have a place somewhere in the middle of the building; thus, the proposition was less favorable than that rejected in 1952. Eliot told the Angelenos "I don't think that will go over"; he knew that "the Club was 'fed up' with similar previous offers". But he did admit "that was a fine lunch".

In the Black

The Club's financial improvement was by and large turned to good purpose, but in 1954 its new-found prosperity had gone to the Directors' collective heads and there were some excesses. For example, on April 15, the Board conferred upon all former Presidents of the Club the privilege of signing for "free" drinks — i.e., their chits would be covered by the Club. Again, the annual meeting dinner followed the example set by Leon de Fremery in 1945 by being complimentary,[10] but without de Fremery's insistence that those who took a free dinner also had to attend the meeting so that in 1954, while 111 members came to dinner, only 80 attended the meeting. But perhaps the most telling evidence that the Club was on easy street was a vote at a special membership meeting on March 24 to increase initiation fees while reducing the maximum number of resident members from 500 to 400.[11] Taking into account the Club's fixed costs and foreseeable future needs, this probably reduced the maximum below the Club's optimum. Whether that was so or not, the vote flouted the lesson of history that, practically speaking, the Club should always welcome qualified new members.

Unquestionably, the Club was riding the crest of a wave at this time, attracting new young members like Tindall Cashion (1953) and Frederick O. Johnson, then newly arrived from Southern California (1954). Cashion remembered of the era that any night of the week: "you could come up...after work and the members' bar would be full. We had probably anywhere from fifteen to thirty people up here having cocktails". The Club's more formal events, such as 1954's Bastille Day dinner and its "Night in Spain", were variations of the sort of occasion that the Club had earlier enjoyed under the name "epicure nights".

Squash continued to be an important recreation of some members. At the urging of Games Committee Chairman Donald L. Colvin, the Board on October 10, 1955 budgeted for $250 per annum for prizes for various squash tournaments, joined the Pacific Coast Squash Racquet Association for $25, and for another $25 helped sponsor an exhibition match by Hashin Khan and Azzem Khan of Pakistan, two internationally known players.

Sending in a Marine

The only cause of discord in an otherwise exceptionally harmonious decade was filling the position of manager. For example in 1953, the Club tried three men in that position,[12] the last one of whom, R.E. Bayley, remained until June of 1956 when John C. Schaefer was appointed to replace him. Thus began a remarkable love-hate relationship between employer and employee.

Schaefer had been a marine in the war, serving through several campaigns in its Pacific theatre. He applied marine precepts to running the Club, ruled the staff with an iron hand and could be ruthless in his dealings with underlings and suppliers. Some members thought he had entirely too much influence on Club affairs, such as who was to be on the Board, or even Club President. By nature he was not deferential; and there were times when he ignored the wishes of the members, as when in 1972 he gave a newspaper interview, in utter disregard of the proper protocol in a Club which had always fought shy of publicity.[13]

On the other hand, some members admired Schaefer. According to past-President Tindall

Cashion, the Christmas parties of the 1950s and 1960s, organized by Schaefer, were superb. Moreover, the Board thought enough of him in 1959 to boost his salary to $1,000 a month — a huge increase. And he was a survivor: he served longer than any other manager in the Club's history. For better or worse, his influence during his long tenure was great and sometimes decisive in the turbulent sixties and seventies.

Notes

1. Two of the six that were retained have disappeared. The four original Audubon prints have been supplemented by high-grade reproductions so that the third-floor dining room has a total of thirteen Audubons on display.

2. The House Committee had recommended a plan devised by member A.C. Mayer to expend up to $77,000.

3. The seven universities were: Columbia, Cornell, Michigan, University of Oregon, Princeton, University of Virginia and University of Washington. All of them date their foundation before that of the Club.

    Today, the Club would not have the window space to commemorate all the various colleges and universities from which its members come.

4. This painting is now displayed in the lobby of the Club.

5. In 1972 the gallery was named after Henry Hardy, to his great pleasure.

6. Of two one-bedroom units and three studios.

7. A complicated arrangement was worked out by which the Graces would buy the property and put it in the trusteeship of Pacific Title Insurance Company, which in turn would then sell the building to the Club. These arrangements nearly aborted when Mrs Grace died before the purchase was complete. Her estate was frozen by the probate courts for some months, but member Chauncey McKeever was able to untangle this mess so that by April 1953 the Club owned the property.

8. See chapter 3, pp. 21-22 supra.

9. The Club's experience in 1952 almost exactly parallels that of the Vancouver Club in 1974. Developers proposed building a skyscraper on the Vancouver Club's site and giving it the two top floors. The proposition was turned down after its Premises Committee concluded "we're better off in our own building". Roy 1989, p.189.

10. However, this was not automatic: the Board voted upon it from year to year in the April preceding the annual meetings of 1954 and 1955.

11. At the time, the Club had 550 members total, of whom 370 were regular resident members.

12. At the beginning of the year, a Mr Bradley held the position, but he was terminated before the May annual meeting. (At the 1953 annual meeting, some members tried to obtain an increase of the two weeks' vacation pay awarded to Bradley on his dismissal, but the Board was opposed and nothing came of the movement).

    At the April 30 meeting of the Board, Walter Schroeder was appointed to the post. One of his first acts was to fire the chef in May for incompetence. Schroeder had another man in mind to fill the vacancy thus created, but somehow he never got hired and the Club was without a chef for months, until Schroeder himself resigned in September.

    He was replaced in October by R.E. Bayley, who was to be paid $650 a month, and who lasted until June of 1956.

13. After Schaefer's interview, the entire staff was reminded that it was not at liberty to answer questions from the press about Club affairs. This was merely a reiteration of a long-standing policy. However, the press – not liking any source of information to be curtailed – made much of this reminder, and when Time-Life Books' San Francisco volume of its *Great Cities of the World* series appeared, its only statement about the Club was that its employees were under orders not to talk to the press! Id., p.40.

CHAPTER 9

The Sixties

Although the fiscal health of the fifties continued into the sixties, money was not as flush as before and in consequence some of the excesses of the 1950s were undone, notably the reduction of the maximum number of permissible resident members to 400 in 1954. In 1961, it was increased to 420. In 1965, the Board increased the limit no less than three times, so that by December it was at 440. By October 1967, the by-laws were changed to allow up to 500 regular members. The incentive for change was the Club's need for added revenues; the Board's action in 1955 had the defect of restricting the Club's ability to control its income. Underlying the vacillations on membership was a lack of consensus about the Club's optimum size.

Why did the Club experience increasing financial stringency during the sixties? There were two elements: first, inflation, including escalating labor costs; and second, the Boards of the sixties made substantial expenditures while continuing to resist all overtures from would-be developers of the Club's premises.

A number of weapons were used to counteract inflation, apart from raising the Club's membership base. Admission fees were raised in 1960 from $300 to $400 while the nonresident fee went up from $50 to $100. Various assessments were imposed. Then, in June of 1965, the Board imposed a 75 cent guest charge for each occasion a member brought in a

guest or guests, and a $5 charge against a member for issuance of a guest card to his guest. In November of that year, regular members' monthly dues rose 20%, from $20 to $24.

Inflation Erodes the Club's Position

But it was not until the latter part of the decade that inflationary pressures became acute, in part because of the Vietnam war. On March 21, 1967, manager Schaefer warned the Board that if it did not take strong measures, the future of the Club would be in doubt. Although gross sales were up in all departments, expenses had risen faster, with labor costs being the biggest problem; some individual salaries had risen 200% in five years.[1]

In July of 1968, the Board recognized the accuracy of Schaefer's analysis by increasing admission fees for regular members over 32 years old from $500 to $1,000. But it responded less successfully on the other side of the balance sheet in curbing expenditure.

Master of its own House

There was one expenditure in the 1960s which brought universal acclaim: the paying off of the debt to the Stanford trustees in the spring of 1962.[2] At last, the Club was master of its own house. At the annual meeting, the financial vice-president of Stanford University, Kenneth Cuthbertson, expressed the congratulations of the trustees. There was a mortgage-burning ceremony attended by some long-time members.[3] This significant event did not, however, mean that the Club could be complacent about its finances; despite the discharge of the mortgage, assessments and dues continued to rise, partly because of continuing improvements around the clubhouse and partly because of protracted and ill-fated negotiations for an interest in the apartment house next door at 830 Powell Street.

No less than four major improvement projects took place in the sixties. They were: creating a new drinking and dining area in the basement; renovation of the fourth floor bar; creation of the small garden fronting onto California Street in which Hermes was placed; and conversion of the old pool and billiards room into a conference room.

Schaefer's Folly

The initiative to utilize the basement came from the Club's manager. It had always been underutilized and was now a virtually wasted asset. It was much bigger than could conceivably be needed by the Club for laying down wine. Furthermore, very few members lived at the Club by the early 1960s and therefore the trunk room was not as necessary as it had been; and its only other function was storage of Hermes. Because of the Club's sloping site on the California Street hill, the basement — in spite of its name — is not subterranean space. On its eastern side it is entirely above ground level and therefore more suitable for occupation than most basements. Some action had been taken on it before the end of the 1950s; but the sixties were to see a much more grandiose expansion. Finishing the basement would provide new social space and solve some scheduling difficulties. When John Schaefer had seen this opportunity back in 1957, his creation had become known as "Schaefer's Folly" — but with the installation of a splendid old wooden bar from Nevada in the basement's southeastern corner, it became a popular venue for members[4] — and thus Schaefer's "folly" turned out not to be so foolish after

all. Perhaps because he had been vindicated by the initial opening of the basement, by March 1963, Schaefer proposed a further great expansion into the space with a dining area which would have a capacity approaching that of the third floor. His proposal fell upon sympathetic ears and on May 20 the Board under President Chauncey McKeever approved expenditure of $17,000 to complete the project. By September, it had been accomplished.

There is no question but that the basement was a popular rendezvous throughout the rest of the sixties, the whole of the seventies and the early part of the eighties. But there were to be grave problems with the structural soundness of the basement in the later eighties. Furthermore, its facilities, although different in style, were essentially duplicative of what the Club offered on other floors: and some, at least, of the custom which went to the basement was diverted there from the more formal space upstairs.

From Schaefer's Folly to Hermes' Garden

In a sense, Schaefer's folly led to Hermes' garden; the use of the basement space displaced Hermes from the storage area to which it had been consigned. Schaefer had it dumped outside in Miles Court, the alley behind the Club, where, recalled Henry Hardy, "it was very much in the way of deliveries and garbage pick-up". In 1965, Hardy suggested that Hermes be displayed in the small area between the squash courts and California Street. The Board agreed and appropriated $1,500 for landscaping and a chainlink fence. Later, a bronze plaque was put nearby, explaining who Hermes was. The result was that the Club won a city beautification award. However, as will be seen in chapters 10 and 11, Hermes was not to remain completely undisturbed in his own garden.

Renovation of the fourth floor members' bar was long overdue, but it was a touchy subject. Although the wallpaper was peeling, the metal fixtures were rusting, the ceiling was dark and cracked, the woodwork needed refinishing, the carpet was soiled and worn and the furniture was falling apart, its *habitues* were wary of improvements; they liked the bar the way it was. Still, President Tindall Cashion spruced the place up, while ensuring that it remained recognizably the bar it had always been. Cashion was greatly relieved when, after the redecoration was accomplished, a member commented to him: "You didn't change it a bit. You didn't hurt it a bit. You did all this beautiful work and it's still the same". So was voiced an ever-present element of Club spirit.

The last project was achieved in 1967-68 through the generosity of a Board member, Dr Frank Pierce. Use of the billiards room had diminished substantially while a desire for a small fourth floor dining room had frequently been expressed. It was decided that conversion of the pool room into a private dining room, to be called the directors' room, but available to other members when not in use by the Directors, would be a good utilization of the space.

In Vino Felicitas

A happy inspiration of the sixties was the formation of a Wine Committee under the chairmanship of George Hale in 1963. Although the original plans of the clubhouse had included a wine room, the Club had made no consistent effort to lay down good wines, in spite of the potential for capital appreciation. As Frederick O. Johnson, a member of the original committee recollected, the manager knew little about wines and yet wine was a major local product in which there was increasing interest. This Committee has been among the most active and enthusiastic ever since.

The Committee selects the wines available in the clubhouse, including the house wines, and some of its selections are offered under the Club's own label.

The 830 Powell Street Controversy, Part One

Alas, not all was harmony in the sixties. The end of the decade saw the beginning of a controversy which did not end until 1971 about the Club's attempt to acquire 830 Powell Street, the apartment building next door. In 1919, the Club had declined to buy this building for $22,500. Now, it was going to rue the day: a protracted and unsuccessful attempt to

The private label used on bottles of the Club's "centennial selection" Chardonnay.

purchase the property created more divisiveness and ill-feeling in the Club than perhaps at any time in its history, almost proving Lincoln's aphorism that a house divided against itself cannot stand. It poisoned the atmosphere of three annual meetings (in 1969, 1970 and 1971) and its outcome was that the Club ultimately spent a lot of money with little to show for it.

At first, the matter revived as a Club issue only collaterally. What brought the question back onto the Board's agenda was not a Club desire to expand as a landlord (123 Joice Street was already causing more trouble than it was worth), but to control the alley behind the Club, Miles Court.

In 1904, Miles Court had been declared a private right of way, but on May 16, 1961 after questions had been raised about its use for car parking by non-members, the Board stated its understanding that it "belonged to the owners of adjacent property abutting on the Street. We are therefore unable to preclude use of same to such persons. A letter stating the facts is to be placed in a permanent file for future reference". The Club did own some of the property adjacent to Miles Court, but not all of it: 830 Powell was the principal property it did not own. Since it had become the Board's belief that control of 830 Powell meant control of Miles Court, there was a revival of interest in its acquisition.

Much of the friction that developed regarding the use of Miles Court by outsiders reflected a parking problem. Street parking was becoming more and more difficult on Nob Hill and the Club had no parking lot of its own. Thus, members who drove to the Club wanted to use the space on Miles Court, and — frustrated when they found it full, as they did with increasing frequency — they were deterred from using the Club. The Board had long recognized the reality that some of the decline in the Club's utilization, especially in the evening, was attributable to parking difficulties. As early as 1962, member John Walker had proposed that the Club, when it rebuilt the squash courts (as it was to do in the 1970s), incorporate into its plans a parking garage for 50 automobiles — and the Board adopted the proposal in April, although it was soon found impracticable.[5]

Nothing further happened until 1968, when the owner of 830 Powell died leaving the property to the American Cancer Society, which asked $250,000 for it. The Club then heard that the Fairmont Hotel had offered $500 more than the Society's asking price and deputed three members[6] to investigate further. Then, on March 10, 1969, President William B. MacColl, Jr. and Board member Gregory S. Stout met with Ben Swig, the Fairmont's owner. Swig said he wanted 830 Powell to protect his hotel's view and would be interested in knowing if the Club was ever to dispose of its clubhouse. He went on to say that if he acquired 830 Powell he would be prepared to sell the Club a half interest. At a Board meeting held immediately after the meeting with Swig, it was resolved to follow up on Swig's offer "because the Club does not have the resources to bid against the

Fairmont Hotel Corporation, [and] a one-half interest would be better than nothing": half a loaf is better than none. The Directors acted on the assumption that "Presumably, Mr Swig would go along with closing the alley behind the Club".

All this was done despite "a limited time in which to secure details" and with an air of urgency. By the time the Board met again on March 25, there was already some opposition to the earlier resolution from Vice-President Frank Pierce. Nevertheless, the Club signed a contract with Swig on April 6. This was soon seen by Henry Hardy who concluded, with Pierce, that not only did it not address the Miles Court issue adequately, "but it could not be binding because a compact of this magnitude exceeded the Board's powers and required membership approval". Within four days, the Board was threatened with a lawsuit and by April 21, it had conceded that some language in the agreement with Swig needed tightening and that an alternative way of dealing with Miles Court was to bring proceedings to quiet title and fix rights under the McEnerney Act.[7] But this was not enough to pacify the opposition, especially when it learned that the Board had already paid $25,000 to Swig to seal the bargain. This revelation was especially ill-timed because the Club's annual meeting was only a month away.

The annual meeting on May 21 was contentious. In a two-hour debate, the opposition expressed its belief that the Board had overstepped its authority and that the agreement with Swig was anyway imprudent. When it became clear that no consensus would emerge, "President MacColl heard a motion, duly seconded, that the meeting be adjourned". This passed, but only just, by a vote of 63 to 61: some opponents of the Board saw this as evidence that it was unwilling to include the membership at large in the decision-making process. Thereupon, the opposition sent members its argument that the whole exercise of the Board was unnecessary since the Club already owned half of Miles Court, and demanding that the $25,000 paid to Swig be retrieved.[8]

The Board was evidently in a dither. At its meeting of May 27, it appointed new President John Lewis and immediate past-President MacColl to go and see Swig to explain why no progress had been made on the Club's side. At the same time, it appointed two subcommittees on 830 Powell, one to report on finances and the other on legal aspects. Both these reports were to disapprove the Board's action, although the financial report underwent an extraordinary *volte face*. John Clow of the financial committee made a first report which, according to the Board's Minutes and notwithstanding that the Club had already parted with $25,000, found that the 830 Powell transaction would have no adverse financial effect. Within two days, Clow had submitted a second report with a contrary viewpoint. Not only did it concede that "830 Powell Street cannot be operated on an economically satisfactory basis", but it stated:

The present transaction does not appear to achieve the objective of (a) closing Miles Alley and obtaining clear title to it, and (b) obtaining

an interest in 830 Powell Street on an economically satisfactory basis.[9]

By June 19, 1969, the Board conceded in its Minutes that "the agreement with the Fairmont on 830 Powell is an imperfect one as it now exists"; and by August 8, it had voted to follow the opposition's recommendation that the Club bring a McEnerney Act suit to determine what its rights were in Miles Court and retained attorney Philip Diamond to pursue the matter.[10] And on September 30, 1969, the Board announced that it was seeking to withdraw from the agreement entered with the Fairmont. To all intents and purposes, therefore, the opposition had prevailed and it would have been natural for the controversy to end. Alas, however, it had merely abated and had yet to flare up at its fiercest as an inauspicious opening to the seventies.

Notes

1. By the fall of 1968, the Club was dealing with five separate unions. Only fifteen years before, the employees were completely ununionized.

2. Hindsight makes the reasons for the Club's joy less self-evident than it was then: the loan was at 4 1/2% fixed, well below the rate of inflation, and therefore it was cheap money. But, of course, there was a great symbolic significance in paying off the mortgage.

3. They included Clay Miller, Frank Adams, Chauncey McKeever, Harry E. Miller, Jr., Churchill Peters, S.V. Beckwith, Jr., Charles E. Noble and Frank Chambers.

4. A persistent piece of Club lore asserts that until this time, the cobbled floor of the old Stanford stables was visible in the basement. However, the excavations of the late 1980s uncovered only a few individual, unlaid cobblestones.

5. The proposal was dropped on June 18, 1962, with the Board citing the need to acquire more property on Joice Street as the greatest obstacle.
The problem of parking has plagued many city clubs,

An example is the Sutter Club of Sacramento which opened its own multi-story parking facility in 1986. The Club's historian commented that following this, "the turn-around for the Sutter Club was remarkable in its scope and speed". Comstock 1989, p.221.

6. Francis Barnes, Chauncey McKeever and Southall Pfund.

7. This statute was passed after the 1906 earthquake to allow quieting of dubious real property titles. It is named after Garret William McEnerney, who was a member of the Club: see volume 2 of *San Francisco: Its Builders Past and Present* (1913), pp.277-278.

8. According to Henry Hardy (who was a leader of the opposition throughout) the Board refused to give access to the roster of members' addresses, so that members could be circularized. The opposition compiled its own list.

9. The finance committee's second report raised further objections, oddly (since there was a separate legal subcommittee) of a legal rather than a financial nature. It said that if the acquisition of 830 Powell was achieved, the agreement left the Club's rights after twenty-five years

unclear. Also, the Fairmont Hotel would be able to control the building while unloading half the cost of doing so on the Club "without corresponding benefits and rights".

10. The suit (case no. 44,065) was ultimately won by the Club, with final judgment entered April 15, 1971.

CHAPTER 10

The Contentious Seventies

The 830 Powell Street Controversy, Part Two

The supposition had been at the end of 1969 that the contract with the Fairmont Hotel regarding 830 Powell Street would be rescinded amicably. But on February 10, 1970, President Lewis had to report to his Board that Swig was "not willing to permit the Club to withdraw from the April 6, 1969 agreement and get back the money the Club had paid out". In the light of that, Lewis, together with Director Stout, was "now working with Mr. Swig to obtain an agreement which will give the Club an eventual opportunity for full ownership of 830 Powell Street". Lewis and Stout thought that a McEnerney suit should follow approval of such an agreement.

This incensed the opposition, which wanted no further dealings with Swig and the immediate prosecution of the McEnerney action. It bought pressure to bear so that the McEnerney suit was put in the hands of attorney Philip Diamond in March 1970, but still the Board wanted to treat with Swig. Thus it was that on May 1, 1970, with the annual meeting only a few days away, the opposition distributed a privately printed document which concluded:

A year has gone by. An enormous amount of time and money have been spent with still no

result. It is just as clear now as it was a year ago that the original agreement of April 1969 is invalid and unworkable....If a new agreement is presented, the Club will be faced with an immediate payment of a minimum of twenty thousand...dollars more, plus substantial monthly payments...for a prolonged number of years....How this money is proposed to be raised and the necessity for it are of vital concern to every Member. The Directors should take some positive complete position with respect to 830 Powell Street and submit their proposal for the approval or disapproval of the entire Membership by formal secret ballot before any commitments are made.

Another rocky annual meeting was ensured. At it, a resolution was overwhelmingly passed asking for clarification of the terms of the original agreement with the Fairmont and to have it voted on by the entire membership. If a prompt clarification could not be achieved, the agreement should be rescinded unilaterally and a new committee be established to deal with the issue.

The new President Gregory S. Stout appointed such a committee, the first act of which was to establish an open file in the Club's front office which any member could consult to see the current state of play. Although this pleased the opposition, an unfortunate exchange ensued between Henry Hardy, its spokesman, and the President.[1]

Tempers remained frayed throughout the year and on into 1971. The membership remained bitterly divided, the issue remained hot and a kind of stalemate developed. As the annual meeting of May 19, 1971 approached, the atmosphere was so explosive that the Board passed an unprecedented one-time-only rule banning the sale of alcoholic beverages from 4 pm until the conclusion of the meeting, to help keep emotions in check. As it turned out, the meeting was emotional, but the issue was not 830 Powell!

The new President was to be Frederick O. Johnson who, being professionally engaged in real estate, gave the opposition some hope that the 830 Powell Street mess would be resolved in a businesslike manner. Henry Hardy, although unquestionably in fighting mood, conceded that Johnson was doing his best to extricate the Club and regain the funds expended on the transaction: and indeed by December the Club was free of it. Thus, at the annual meeting, although many members were frustrated about the matter, Johnson's election to the Presidency was seen by both sides as a good one and relatively little was said about it, except for a status report.

However, the poison of the 830 Powell controversy had spilled over into entirely unrelated questions, such as Club admissions, and they became the main focus of the meeting. It was a symptom of how strained relationships within the Club had become; suspicion and paranoia were in the air.

The Club's by-laws had always been free of ethnic or racial restrictions. But civil rights were continually in the news in the sixties and it was therefore more or less inevitable that the Club would get involved somehow. And sure enough, in the mid-1960s, an Episcopal minister broadcast an accusation on radio station KFRC that the Club, along with the Bohemian, the Olympic and the Pacific Union, was discriminatory.[2] Unpleasant though this was, it had little significance until in 1970, past-President Richard Ernst (1956-1957) thought he detected discrimination in the Club.

Earlier in the year, he had proposed a candidate for membership who had been rejected by the Admissions Committee. Ernst, incensed, believed that the Committee's decision stemmed from prejudice and at the annual meeting he said so. He then made two dramatic motions. The first was to affirm the Club's policy not to withhold or grant membership on prejudicial grounds and the second would have required that members of the Admissions Committee should take an oath to honor that policy. This was a direct attack on the Committee; he asserted that "the membership committee had failed to live up to the Club's by-laws and hence he was stressing the use of the loyalty oath upon taking office".[3]

A number of prominent members spoke against Ernst's motions, including outgoing President Stout. Finally an amendment to the loyalty motion was moved and adopted:

It has been and shall be the continued policy of the Club that membership not be denied, delayed, or granted on the basis of any consideration of race, creed, color, national or ethnic origin or religious or political beliefs.

Not only did this amendment eliminate the loyalty oath proposal, but it was in the more palatable form of an affirmation of existing policy. Ninety-one members voted in favor. So ended a very unpleasant controversy, ultimately to everyone's satisfaction: later in the 1970s, Ernst himself served as a member of the Admissions Committee.

After that embattled annual meeting, attention reverted to 830 Powell. On June 29, the special real estate committee set up in May, 1970 reported once again its opinion that the 830 Powell Street transaction, as an investment, simply did not make sense. Johnson decided to cut the Club's losses and end the arrangement with Swig before further economic and institutional damage was done. He therefore ordered that the April 1969 agreement be terminated, that any and all commitments made since be terminated, and that payments made to the Fairmont should be written off on the Club's books. By December 16, 1971, all the necessary papers to accomplish these aims had been signed and the whole sorry episode had ended. It was small consolation that, as a result of the McEnerney Act suit, the Club did emerge with full rights over Miles Court.

Over a three year period, many good members had had their feelings hurt, and much time and money (perhaps $50,000) had been spent. Why? The short answer was that a tenant of 830 Powell Street persistently asserted a right to park his automobile behind the Club to the annoyance of members looking for a parking space. After some incidents of vandalism, hostilities escalated to such an extent that a few members with access to the Board became so obsessed that it took four Presidential terms for the Club to turn its attention back to its main business.

Back to Ordinary Business

Inflation, already serious in the late sixties, worsened in the seventies to such a degree that federal wage and price controls were imposed. Even before then, however, the Club had felt the chill wind of rising prices to such an extent that the first Club administration of the decade, that of John Lewis (1969-70), took a radical step by changing the Club's tax status from non-profit to for-profit. This opened the way for the Club to tap new sources of income. With nonprofit status, the Club was limited by law to making a maximum of 15% of its income from non-members and its accounts indicated that the 15% limit would soon be reached, if it had not been already.[4]

The source of this outside income reflected two considerable changes in Club financing and policy. One was the decision, implemented in 1978 when the overnight rooms were completely renovated, that the Club would no longer accommodate permanent residents — an abandonment of one of its original *raisons d'etre*. Yet, in its picturesque building opposite the Club, on the south side of California Street, the San Francisco Residence Club has continued to prosper by providing permanent and semi-permanent rooms of exactly the kind no longer available at 800 Powell. After renovation, the Club's principal opportunity to generate new income was in renting its rooms to outsiders.[5]

The other change was that the Club began to encourage use of its facilities by outside groups sponsored by a member. For many years, a select number of outside organizations had been permitted to hold functions at the Club. For obvious historical reasons, the Harvard Club was allowed to hold its meetings at the clubhouse. The Hughes Club had met on Club premises in the teens of the century. Since 1935, the Club had hosted the annual Oxford and Cambridge boat race dinner; San Francisco's Economic Roundtable had held its breakfast meetings at the Club beginning in 1936; a local literary society, the Roxburghe Club, had met at 800 Powell during the 1950s; and many of the San Francisco Bachelors' functions have taken place at the Club. But in the seventies, the list of associations using the premises greatly expanded.

Two years after the adoption of for-profit status, in May, 1972, a Board study of the economic consequences of the change confirmed that it had been advantageous and the Club continues to be a for-profit entity to this day.

But for-profit status does not guarantee making a profit. And the Club was in a far from buoyant financial state. Members' use of the Club was diminishing: more of them than before lived outside the city and the membership in general was patronizing the Club less. In consequence, in December 1970, the Board introduced a new policy: each regular member would be billed a minimum of $15 per month, regardless of whether he had charged that amount for food or drink. The policy was designed to increase revenues and encourage greater use of the Club, but was more successful in the former aim than the latter.

Labor Costs and the Club Institute

The greatest cause of the Club's financial shortfall was increasing labor costs, which in the fiscal year 1970-71 alone rose $16,000. Not even John Schaefer, who had an aptitude for labor negotiations, could hold back the tide. Under him, relationships with the Hotel and Restaurant Employees' and Bartenders' Union Local 2 had been mostly quiescent, but latterly, he could not work any magic. His last "victory" in labor negotiations was to keep wage increases down to 5 1/2% and this was possible only because of the introduction of federal price and wage guidelines.

By 1973 when, for reasons of poor health, Schaefer retired after seventeen years of service, the nation was wracked by inflation and a different approach was necessary. On Schaefer's replacement by the Club's popular dining room *maitre d'hotel*, Patrick Jones, President Richard Nixon's wage and price controls were in effect: but once these were rescinded, union pressure was felt very strongly and on June 1974, in the face of it, the Club joined the Club Institute (at $300 plus $40 per month thereafter) in order that it would handle labor negotiations in the future. By July, the Institute had agreed on an annual 7 1/2% wage increase for employees for three years. Inevitably, this meant a further dues increase for Club members: in April, 1975, monthly dues for a regular member went up from $35 to $40. The pattern of the future was established. When the collective bargaining agreement of July 1974 expired, the result of the new negotiations was another round of increases in Club fees of various kinds: the admission fee for regular members over 30 years of age increased to $1,250. In January, 1978, the one-time fee for life membership was doubled to $5,000; and in January 1979, monthly dues for the Club's 477 resident members who were above 30 years old went up twenty-five per cent, from $40 to parity with the Bohemian Club at $50.[6]

These conditions were not unique to the University Club; many other clubs were feeling the pinch. In the ebb and flow of clubland, the seventies were a period of ebb. In several other clubs in the city, it was said that one had "to sit and watch the entire membership die off". That was not true at the University Club, but it had no room for complacency: in spite of its much-vaunted attempts to attract younger men, by 1979, those under 30 accounted for less than 5% of the total resident membership.

The Club certainly tried to make itself attractive. The fourth floor art exhibits were a refreshing source of interest every month. The Club's handsome library, too long neglected, got some attention: in 1972, a group of members contributed $1,475 towards its recataloguing and in 1979, Thomas E. Woodhouse

inaugurated a circulating collection of modern books. In 1978, member John B. Stuppin revived the Club's musical interests by arranging what Henry Hardy called "extravangazas", put on by professional musical groups.

Appealing to somewhat different tastes, the freshly installed wine cellar bar became a favorite spot for members.[7] And by a crooked path, an offshoot of the Club's "one-and-a-half" nights became one of the most popular annual events in the Club's calendar: boxing night.

One-and-a-half nights had continued without interruption since they were inaugurated in the 1930s but by 1975, as one of their founders, Chauncey McKeever noted, not all was well. They had degenerated from being pleasant introductory receptions for potential new members to a point where they had become an open house at which members of the public with sufficient lack of scruple could come and drink at the Club's expense. The Board, aware of this problem, tried to deal with it in March by adding a buffet supper after the cocktails and changing the name of the occasion to "Club Night": as before, the emphasis was on inviting potential new members. Then in December 1977, the Entertainment Committee, inspired by "smokers" the Club had held before the days of television, arranged that these evenings should also feature amateur boxing contests. These were an immediate success. Members took to wearing dinner jackets and smoking cigars as they watched the bouts, creating a Hogarthian scene reminiscent of George Bellows' 1909 painting, now in the National Gallery, entitled "Both Members of the Club". The popularity of these spectacles was such that boxing night became an event in its own right, separate from the one-and-a-halfs. It remains an annual fixture, usually oversubscribed, to this day.

New Squash Courts

Sports in the Club got a tremendous boost in the seventies, beginning in February 3, 1972, when the Board hoped that "new, more varied athletic facilities" would attract a "sizable group of new members, most of whom would be among the younger age group". Initially, the Board had in mind not only new squash courts with a steam room, sauna, gymnasium equipment, showers and lockers, but tennis courts and a swimming pool too. Expansion of such a grand scale did not take place, but nevertheless the project as finally put to the membership was large, with an anticipated cost of $250,000, well over the $100,000 limit set by the by-laws on the Board's discretion.

Some opposition to the Board's plans developed; there were older members who felt that it might change the Club's character from social to athletic, and others who felt the large expenditure would benefit only a minority of members.

Under Club rules, it was necessary for two-thirds of the resident and life members to vote in favor of the scheme. In the event, at a special meeting held on March 7, 1973, 347 members voted in favor, with only 71 against. By any standards, this was a striking mandate to go ahead. Two weeks later, the Board, under the Presidency of Dwight M. Cochran, Jr., approved a $4.75 assessment on the membership to help fund the project. By December 11, a building contract had been let to Floyd Svensson of Orinda at under $200,000, for a two-story wood frame structure with lockers but without most of the other facilities originally envisioned.

A little over two years later, a gala opening of the building was held. On February 18, 1976, cocktails were served in the wine cellar as a preliminary to two exhibition matches. The first pitted Alex Eichmann of the Pensinula Squash Club, a four-time Pacific Coast champion, against Tom Dashiell of the Olympic Club, the top rated amateur in northern California. The second game was a doubles match played on "the only double court in California". Dinner followed in 800 Powell's main dining room. Thus were the new facilities off to an auspicious start. Within the first year of their opening, the Club had hosted two major tournaments and many lesser events. Squash Committee Chairman Murray Smith reported that members had rented 117 lockers, guest fees were being collected and the squash facilities had become a money-maker for the Club.

In 1978 the Club hosted the 57th Lapham Cup tournament between Canada and the United States, easily financing the event through voluntary contributions. A $100 a plate black tie dinner-dance at the Club was held as a fund raiser, the sponsors of which received reserved seats to all matches.

Hermes Lost and Found

A distraction from the Club's official program was the theft, on the night of Thursday, December 19, 1974, of Hermes from its California Street resting place. This heist was no mean achievement; the statue was, as Henry Hardy put it, "400 pounds of awkwardness", set more than three feet below sidewalk level and enclosed behind a locked six foot chain fence: no one ever discovered how it was removed. The disappearance was reported to the police, but they showed almost no concern; statues were disappearing from Golden Gate Park at the same time and apparently being melted down for their scrap value. In default of official law enforcement, a publicity campaign was mounted and on January 9, 1975, Herb Caen opened his *Chronicle* column with an appeal for Hermes' return. In response to this, the Club received a telephone call saying that one Gabriel Sheridan knew where the statue was: he had been at a friend's house when he saw it "with a fur coat draped to conceal it" in the living room. The friend explained that he had purchased the statue from an antique dealer and planned to sell it in Florida at a profit. Sheridan said that he could arrange the return of the statue without any money changing hands if Hardy could arrange for its pick-up the next day, no questions asked. This was managed and the statue was recovered virtually undamaged. By January 14, Herb Caen proclaimed: "this sterling column gets results" and that Hermes had been saved "from a fate worse than death. Miami Beach".

Notes

1. President Stout said that a rescission notice had been served on Ben Swig on September 9, and Hardy said that it had not. And the opposition, of which Hardy was a leading member, sent another report to members, accusing the President of neglecting his duties and ignoring the instructions of the annual meeting relating to 830 Powell.

2. "Choose Your Obscenities", by Canon Robert Cromey, Vicar of St. Aidan's, San Francisco, October 12, 1965. His list of clubs was almost identical to Miss Sally Stanford's: see chapter 6, footnote 2, p.51 supra. Cromey's argument was that "Christian clergymen and laymen....who belong to these clubs without challenging these policies are guilty of obscenity...." In accordance with a long-standing policy against press releases, the Club did not respond to this attack.

3. The Club's Admissions and Membership Committees are different, but apparently in the heat of debate they were confused at the annual meeting.

4. This did not necessarily mean a healthy state of finances: the percentage rose because the income from members was falling.

5. Initially sponsored by a member. But in 1975-76, President George G. Skou greatly expanded the network of reciprocal arrangements with other clubs, with the intention of encouraging their members to use the University Club's rental rooms, dining rooms and bar. Of course, University Club members were extended similar courtesies when they traveled.

6. The seventeen regular members between 25 and 29 years of age had their dues increased from $27 to $35 and those few between 21 and 24 were boosted from $15 to $20.

These membership figures reveal how relatively little impact the Club's policy of encouraging younger members has had in later days.

7. Before his retirement, John Schaefer boasted to the Sunday San Francisco *Examiner and Chronicle* that it generated $19,000 per annum in revenue. He was much criticised for airing the Club's private business in the press and this cast a shadow over his last months as manager.

CHAPTER 11

Modern Times

The Battle of the Sexes

From its foundation, the University Club had always been an association of men. Not only had it no female members, but for a long period (1909-1942) women were totally banned from its clubhouse. During most of the Club's existence, there was no demand for the admission of women and when the issue briefly surfaced in the sixties it submerged quickly. Even in the seventies, it was not to the fore. But in the eighties, proposals to admit women led to protracted debates, conducted at both idealistic and practical levels.

Beginning in World War II, there had been intermittent relaxation of the rules against admitting women as guests, but it was not until 1965 that the first inquiries about membership for women were made: the Club responded simply by pointing out that the Club was for men only. Additionally, in September of 1966, women were admitted to the second floor Cable Car room after 5.30 pm. Nothing else happened until seven years later, when debate was reopened at the Board meeting of February 27, 1973 by Director Thomas A. Wright, who called attention to the fact that while "ladies were permitted to attend parties in the Cable Car room" they "were not permitted to use the elevator for purposes of reaching the Cable Car room". After considerable discussion, the Board determined that in future the

ladies should be allowed to use the elevator.

Again, there was a period of calm. But after three years, a bigger discussion began about whether ladies should be allowed as guests for lunch in the third-floor dining room. The matter was finally put to the 1976 annual meeting and after an affirmative vote, the dining room was opened to women at lunch, beginning August 16. This was reported in the December 12 issue of *Business Week*. After making reference to several San Francisco clubs, it noted:

Another San Francisco club, the University Club, appears to be effecting change step-by-step. It recently opened its business luncheons to women, but it does not yet offer them memberships. "Social change takes a a little time," explains Charles La Follette, club president and a vice president of Crown Zellerbach.

This passage angered some members because of its description of the Club's luncheon service as "business" luncheons. It seemed to adopt an assumption made by the women's liberation movement that, by definition, business was conducted across the luncheon tables of all-male clubs. This rankled because, whatever the position elsewhere, it was not true of the University Club; action had been taken to prevent use of the Club's main dining room for business. Early in 1966, for instance, when the Board thought that business interests were obtruding into the dining room, the Minutes of its meeting of February 23 recorded:

> There was considerable discussion concerning the increasing use of [the Club's main dining room, lounges and members' bar] for obvious business purposes which was found to be inimical to the friendly social atmosphere which is characteristic of the University Club. Accordingly, it was suggested and approved that a brief reminder should be sent out to the Membership with the bills suggesting that in the event members desired business meetings, the private rooms should be used.

This was implemented by a rule that no briefcases or business papers of any kind were acceptable in the dining room. When San Francisco *Chronicle* reporter Blake Green wrote an article on the city's clubland, he concluded that accusations concerning business being done in the Club were overstated, observing: "If one attempts to jot down a few notes at the luncheon table at the University Club, the waiter will politely remind the offender that such overt acts of conducting business are not permissible".[1]

At a practical level, the Club's most important self-examination had come in May of 1976, when the United States treasury department started to investigate major banks that paid employee expenses incurred at private clubs. The department took no action, but as *Business Week* commented in the same issue in which it had referred to the University Club's "business luncheons", even the possibility of disallowance of claims for business expenses incurred at single-sex clubs brought changes. In particular, it reported that the San Francisco-based Bank of America "startled more conservative business elements" by announcing "that it would no longer reimburse executives for dues in all-male clubs" and that "Transamerica Corp. recently decided not to hold its board meetings at San Francisco's all-male Pacific Union Club, and...Wells Fargo followed through with a directive that bans bank functions at clubs that exclude women and minorities".

Clearly, the issue was one whose time had come. At 1980's annual meeting, outgoing President William H. Bentley listed a variety of continuing efforts at both federal and state levels to penalize all-male clubs and warned that the issue would not go away. Unsurprisingly, therefore, one of the major actions of his successor, David E. Mundell, was to appoint a committee to conduct a survey of the membership. This would solicit some information about members and their attitudes to admitting women and giving members' wives access to the Club without their husbands.

The very fact of the survey was disliked in some quarters; it was felt that the proper course for proponents of action (on whatever subject) was to bring a proposal onto the floor of the annual meeting and have it voted up or down there. But since a survey committee had been appointed and was going ahead, an unofficial committee was formed by opponents of admitting women, which called itself the Committee to Preserve University Club Traditions. This committee opposed both the admission of female members and the extension of spousal privileges.

The survey was completed on March 31, 1981 and its results were tallied by the Club's auditors. Of 504 surveys sent out, 396 (78.6%) were returned, and the vote was overwhelmingly against admission of female members.[2] Faced with this vote, the special survey committee recommended that no change should be made. The conservative element in the Club had for the time being won a resounding victory. But at the same time the informational aspect of the survey indicated the vulnerability of the Club to government pressure. A full 46% of respondents admitted that their employers paid their membership fees and 20.5% said their employers worked on government contracts. And some governmental agencies, like the state tax board and the liquor control board, could do great harm to the Club. In Sacramento, bills were constantly being introduced to prohibit tax deductions for business expenses incurred at, and even to revoke the liquor licenses of, single-sex clubs.[3] And a municipal ordinance like that with which New York City was already threatening its clubs could be devastating.[4]

Successive Club Presidents, recognizing the vulnerability of the Club, kept a wary eye on developments. Regardless of their personal preferences, they knew that things might go against the Club. Creative solutions were sought: under the Presidencies of both A. Malcolm Post, Jr. (1986-1987) and J. Murray Fox (1987-1988) the Board made overtures to certain all-female clubs about merging, but they were rebuffed[5] and it was forced back to surveys once more: newly elected President Murray Fox appointed a "Membership Qualification Committee" co-chaired by Allen Strand and Ignazio J. Ruvolo. This Committee circulated position papers both pro and con and held two "forums" on the matter before conducting its survey,[6] but by this time not many minds were likely to be changed by arguments.

The faction in favor of women was more optimistic than during the previous surveys because a recent change in the Club's by-laws had replaced the old rule by which action required a two-thirds vote with one by which a simple majority would be enough to admit women. The results, tabulated by Peat, Marwick, Main and Company, were released in January: 57% of those voting were in favor of admitting women. However, the pro-women faction was defeated by another constitutional requirement of the Club: only 364 members had returned ballots and they did not constitute a majority of those eligible to vote.[7] In the light of this, President Murray Fox and the rest of the Board agreed that the issue would have to be put to a vote yet again, but wished to defer until a relevant case then pending before the United States Supreme Court, no. 86-1836, had been decided.

In the meantime, the Board began to consider what the Club could do if the Court's decision turned out to be unfavorable. Apart from allowing women to become members, there seemed to be only one alternative: "privatization". This would mean limiting the membership to 400 and refusing all revenue from outsiders. Board member Kirk Miller estimated that this would cause a $62 to $96 jump in each member's monthly dues.[8] It was thought that the membership would not stand for this, but just in case it was the members' will, contingency plans to privatize were drawn up.

The Annual Autumn Game Dinner, November 6, 1981, inspired some fine calligraphy.

With the Supreme Court decision imminent, President Fox wrote to the membership on April 12 suggesting another vote, causing an immediate flurry of activity. On April 28, thirty of the advocates of admitting women wrote to the Board objecting to privatization and recommending the recasting of the Club's by-laws in "gender neutral" terms so as to clear the way for female membership.[9] On the other

The University Club
of San Francisco
Bulletin   May 1986

Mother's Day Brunch
Sunday May 11, 1986
11:30 a.m.-1:30 p.m.

This year for your pleasure we will offer caricatures, music and songs by the Gadabouts, and other tableside entertainment and surprises. It will be lots of fun for the whole family to honor Mother on her special day in this very enjoyable way.

This great event is always sold out, so be sure to make early reservations by calling 781-0900.

Adults $25.00   Children under 12 $12.00

Cancellations will be charged after May 6th.

Spring Wine Dinner
Friday May 16, 1986

Traditionally the last major social event of the Club's year has been the Annual Spring Wine Dinner. The Wine Committee is pleased to announce that this will be held Friday evening, May 16th.

This occasion is intended to highlight several of the most attractive and interesting wines from the Club's extensive cellar. As usual, these wines will be served in context of one of Chef Scot Horrobin's fine dinners.

This formal evening is open to members, their ladies, and guests. We'd particularly like to encourage new members to take this opportunity to become acquainted with the excellent capabilities of our dining room, and it is also a good way to introduce potential new members to the club.

Please mark the date and make your reservations with the club office, phone 781-0900.

Black Tie $40.00 per cover

Reservations Limited   No Cancellations
to 50 couples   after May 12th

Reception 6:45 p.m.   Dinner 8:00 p.m.

4th Annual
Frank Adams Memorial
Trap and Skeet Shoot
Saturday May 17, 1986
Pacific Rod & Gun Club

Members and guests, beginners and experts are invited to attend this informal and enjoyable event. The only cost is a $3.50 fee per round which will be charged to the member's account. Loaner guns and instructions will be available on an informal basis. Prizes will be awarded to the top three shooters in trap and in skeet. Bring your own tailgate picnic. Shooting will begin shortly after 11:00 a.m.

Instructional video tapes by Kay Ohye will be shown on Thursday May 15th at 6 p.m. in the Fourth Floor Lounge. The tapes, covering both trap and skeet, display some excellent camera work and provide a good overview of the basics. Cover charge is a nominal $5.00 per person.

Boxing and Dinner
Marquis of Queensbury Event
Eight Three-Round Bouts
Thursday June 19, 1986

This year decisions will be made and the winners of the fights announced. Make your bets, gentlemen!

Cocktails 5:30-7:00 p.m.
Dinner with Wine 7:00 p.m.
Boxing 8:00 p.m.

Members and Limited Number of Male Guests
$25.00 Per Cover
Black Tie Optional

Cancellations will be charged after June 16th
Entertainment Committee

Front page of the Club Bulletin, *announcing four of the Club's most popular annual events.*

side, the Committee to Preserve University Club Traditions asked: "are they entitled to a new vote every year until they win? Two votes a year? More?"

On June 20, after an annual meeting at which Ignazio Ruvolo was elected President but before a new ballot was held, the Supreme Court decision was rendered, upholding the New York City ordinance which had been the pattern of San Francisco's. Shortly thereafter, San Francisco's city attorney, Louise Renne, announced that her special assistant, George Riley had been assigned "exclusively" to enforcement of San Francisco's ordinance.

This forced a renewed look at privatization, since the Club was still not admitting women. The group in favor of admitting them asserted that privatization

would be financially ruinous; the other side countered that it would not be and that if women were admitted, the Club would incur capital costs in accommodating their needs. President Ruvolo and his Board were never as confident as either side about privatization's economic consequences, despite studies by a committee of financial experts: any forecast was just too speculative.

In default of any other solution, the Board scheduled a special meeting on the subject of admitting women for July 20, and arranged for the preparation of another ballot, this time with an information sheet explaining the Supreme Court opinion and its ramifications. But the Board revised these arrangements shortly after they were announced by canceling the July 20 meeting while allowing the ballot to proceed, believing that another meeting would not only be superfluous but unnecessarily fan the flames of acrimony. Arguably, this cancellation backfired, since it was at once protested by the Committee to Preserve University Club Traditions as an irregularity;[10] the Committee suggested postponing both the meeting and the ballot until the fall.

In the face of this protest, the Board moved cautiously. Although the majority of directors thought there had been enough debate and the cancellation of the meeting did not invalidate the ballot, they did not want to inflame the Club still further. They therefore asked the auditors to open and tally the ballots to determine whether one side or the other had won decisively without disclosing which side, if any. The Board was informed that one side had obtained a 79% vote. On that information, on August 29, the Board voted 5 to 2 to validate the election. Only then was the result revealed: 408 members had voted, 323 of them in favor of allowing women to become members and 85 wanting privatization. On September 6, President Ruvolo made a public statement and the next day a *Chronicle* headline read "S.F. University Club to Admit Women". In December 1988, Cecilia Herbert became the Club's first woman member.

Like all revolutions, this one had its costs.[11] During the controversy, members on both sides of the fence resigned in protest or disgust. In the face of the decision to admit women, more resigned, although this reason was unequivocally articulated by only two members. However the resignations are tallied, there were a relatively small number considering how volatile the issue was. On the other hand, throughout it all, the Club had not only survived, but continued to function.

The Continuing Life of the Club

The admittedly great change when the Club went "co-ed" should not obscure the many other developments of the eighties, only a small selection of which can be chronicled.

A useful innovation of this decade was the publication of the *Club Bulletin*, distributed with members' monthly statements of account, and listing prospective new members, what was going on in the Club and incorporating occasional short articles. In a similar vein, the Club has latterly produced a *Club Calendar* twice a year - a sort of fixture card — which conveniently lists major events scheduled for the forthcoming six months.

A new health awareness affected the Club's dining room and bars, where soft drinks, juices and mineral waters were increasingly in demand. In 1984, President William O. Sumner announced the availability of luncheon menus "stressing the lighter foods favored by today's health-conscious man". While reassuring the membership that "hearty eaters need not despair", he indicated a desire that the Club's meal service refute any reputation of being "an old fashioned 'beef and booze' establishment".[12]

In a similar vein, drinking habits moderated in the eighties. Robert Morris remembered that as late as the 1970s, the afternoon would find fifty or more men in the fourth floor bar enjoying cocktails. In contrast, by the late 1980s, as Chauncey McKeever said: "if there are five people there, it's a crowd".

Health consciousness of a different kind was displayed when, in 1985, the Club hired its first squash professional, John Lau. Squash became even more popular and partly because of his incumbency, the Club attracted several new events, notably an exhibition match of March 17, 1987 between Mark Talbott and Ned Edwards, respectively the number

THE UNIVERSITY CLUB
SAN FRANCISCO
CLUB CALENDAR 1990

MARCH

2	Friday —	*Wine Bar & Chef's Night*
2	Friday —	*Pacific Coast Singles Championship*
8	Thursday —	*Speakers Luncheon*
9	Friday —	*Philharmonia Tafelmusik*
13	Tuesday —	*Singing Luncheon*
15	Thursday —	*Breakfast Dialog*
16	Friday —	*Cal State Doubles Championship*
17	Saturday —	*East Bay Gallery Tour*
21	Wednesday —	*Pacific Mozart Ensemble*
28	Wednesday —	*1-1/2 Night*

APRIL

5	Thursday —	*Breakfast Dialog*
6	Friday —	*Spring Wine Luncheon*
19	Thursday —	*Violin & piano recital*
25	Wednesday —	*Secretaries Day*
25	Wednesday —	*1-1/2 Night*
27	Friday —	*Mixed Dominoes*

MAY

3	Thursday —	*Centennial Grand Gala*
4	Friday —	*Centennial Grand Gala*
13	Sunday —	*Mother's Day Brunch*
16	Wednesday —	*Annual Meeting*
18	Friday —	*Spring Wine Dinner*
19	Saturday —	*Trap Shoot*
23	Wednesday —	*1-1/2 Night*
24	Thursday —	*Brown Bag Theatre*
28	Monday —	*Club Closed - Memorial Day*

JUNE

2	Saturday —	*Wine picnic*
12	Tuesday —	*Singing Luncheon*
14	Thursday —	*Boxing Night*
27	Wednesday —	*1-1/2 Night*

JULY

4	Wednesday —	*Club Closed - Independence Day*
25	Wednesday —	*1-1/2 Night*

AUGUST

Club open for breakfast & lunch only
No Club Functions

Front of Club Calendar.

54th Annual
Oxford-Cambridge Boat Race Dinner
April 24, 1989

University Club
San Francisco

GUEST OF HONOR
Professor John Stevens
Quondam President
Magdalene College, Cambridge

Menu

Beef Consomme

Three Greens Salad

Roast Beef, Au Jus
Yorkshire Pudding
Fresh Garden Vegetables

Trifle

Coffee

University Club Specially Selected Wines

LEFT: *The 54th Annual Oxford-Cambridge Boat Race Dinner. This is one of a number of private functions, held at the clubhouse under the sponsorship of a Club member, year after year.*

RIGHT: *"Our Club Heritage". This flyer from the early 1980s advertises a speakers' event reflecting the Club's renewed interest in its history after years of indifference. This renewal of interest led to the establishment of the Club's oral history project at the Bancroft Library of the University of California. The venerable speakers, Leon de Fremery and I.F. Barreda Sherman, were both prominent in the Club's affairs.*

one and number two ranked professionals in north America.

Another innovation was a speakers' program, introduced in January of 1980, and modeled upon one already in place at the University Club of New York. Speakers such as Alexander P. Potemkin, deputy consul-general of the Soviet Union, addressed the Club at lunch or dinner. Over the eighties, a wide variety of topics has been aired in this format.

A great deal of refurbishing went on in the clubhouse. In 1981, the Henry Hardy art gallery was substantially upgraded and on September 24 a dinner was held to mark the occasion and honor the gallery's eponym. In 1984, during the traditional summer vacation, the clubhouse was closed to members to complete structural work. Then the Board gained approval for a $200,000 improvement project, for redecorating the third floor, repairing the clubhouse roof and purchasing a new elevator.

The greatest project of all was proposed in 1987 under President A. Malcolm Post, Jr., for renovation of the kitchen and basement at an estimated cost of $850,000 — by far the greatest single expenditure ever contemplated by the Club. An open meeting approved the proposal on May 13, but alas, before 1987 was out it became clear that the cost, particularly relating to the basement, had been underestimated. The kitchen was completed, but the basement renovation was suspended and remains uncompleted as the Club enters its second century.

Immediately outside the Club's premises, there were some changes, too. Beginning in 1982, its apartment building on Joice Street was upgraded. As each tenant moved out, the opportunity was taken to renovate and repair the vacated apartment.

A quite different and unplanned change took place when on October 30, 1985, in full view of then President Edward L. Bulkley, Hermes was struck down by a rented sports car of which the driver had lost control on California Street. Luckily, no one was hurt — not even Hermes — and within a week he was back on a repaired foundation.

Nob Hill's trend towards catering to transients rather than permanent residents, discernable as early as the 1920s, took on a new form as apartment

UNIVERSITY CLUB
of San Francisco
presents

OUR CLUB HERITAGE
Vignettes and Assorted Secrets

Wednesday, May 6, 1981
as part of the
Luncheon Lecture Series
Price: $10.00

presented by
F.Barreda Sherman
MEMBER SINCE 1920
HISTORIAN AND AUTHOR
and
Leon F. de Fremery
MEMBER SINCE 1923
AND PRESIDENT
44-45, 45-46, 46-47

THIS IS A MUST
— for the young
a chance to know their club
— for the seniors
a chance to reminisce
— and for all of us
the opportunity to be together

buildings were turned into "time-share" units. The Club joined forces with the Nob Hill Association and other groups twice during the eighties in successfully opposing further detrimental development of the area. The most recent threat, in 1989, was to build a twelve story condominium project on the southeastern corner of California and Powell Streets, the vacant site of the long-since demolished Alta Casa apartment house.

The greatest sadness of the eighties was the almost total loss of the clubhouse's magnificent eastern panorama, from which the Club learned the hard way that "there is no easement to a view". The view had always been a source of particular pride; as late as 1979, the Club's brochure for new members had accurately declared that "behind these doors is one of the finest views in San Francisco". Twice over the years the Club had bought property in an attempt to preserve that view; and many more times it had thwarted plans for commercial development which would obscure the bay. But the ultimate enemy turned out not to be commercial developers but the city which, responding to a huge new wave of immigration into Chinatown, authorized the building in 1982 of the Geen Mun Neighborhood Center and adjoining apartments on the corner of Sacramento and Stockton Streets.

It was an uncomfortable sign that nothing can be relied upon completely or taken for granted; nothing is forever. Perhaps it was with this realization that the Club began to take a renewed interest in its history. This was first manifested by an invitation to Leon de Fremery and I.F. Barreda Sherman, two most venerable members, to speak on "Our Club's Heritage". Then, a committee of past-Presidents organized by President Murray Smith (1983-84) recommended that the Club commemorate its heritage. As a result, the Club funded an oral history archive with the Bancroft Library of the University of California from which much of this *Centennial History* has been derived.

A happier aspect of the 1980s was that in 1982, the Club recruited a fine manager who has steered the Club into its centennial year. In the summer of 1981, manager Patrick Jones left the Club to start a new life in Denver. A long search took place before the Board announced the hiring of Desmond Elder, who was formally introduced to the membership on March 29, 1982. One of the few unanimously held opinions of those who have contributed oral histories to the Bancroft Library is that Elder is probably the best manager the Club has ever had.

And perhaps the happiest aspect of the decade was that the clubhouse sustained almost no damage in the earthquake of Tuesday, October 17, 1989. Almost exactly eighty years after its opening, 800 Powell Street showed a resilience mirroring that of the great Club which it houses.

Notes

1. Unlike some Clubs, the University Club never allowed a ticker tape (showing stock market quotations) on its premises. Compare the Vancouver Club, where one was installed in 1918: see Roy 1989, p.107.

Undoubtedly, some clubs are business-oriented. For instance, the Columbia Club of Indianapolis proclaimed in its membership pamphlet, c.1985:

> The Club has acquired a legendary business role in the community as well as being recognized for its political role. It is said that more business decisions are made every day in the undisturbed privacy of the Club than in the formal office setting.

What many members of San Francisco's University Club resented was the failure to differentiate it from such clubs as the Columbia Club, with widely different policies.

2. The survey was very similar to one sent out in 1977, but revealed a strong swing against admitting women since then. Only 21.7% voted in favor of outright admission of women, while another 14.9% favored admission with some restrictions. A full 60.6% voted flatly "no".

3. One of these, Assembly Bill 184, was opposed in a position paper by the California State Club Association in February 1983, on the ground that it unconstitutionally abridged the right of freedom of association. Later, the constitutional objection swung towards privacy rights.

4. San Francisco adopted an ordinance almost identical to New York City's in November, 1987. It was an unsuccessful constitutional challenge to New York's ordinance that led to the Supreme Court's decision on June 20, 1988 in case no. 86-1836, *New York State Club Assn. Inc.* v. *City of New York*, 487 U.S. 1 (1988).

5. All-female clubs like the Metropolitan Club shared the same interests as all-male clubs, but were not targeted by litigation.

6. A third which had been scheduled was never held because a renovation project completely closed the clubhouse for a month.

7. On January 23, 1988, the San Francisco *Chronicle* misleadingly reported this result under the headline "University Club of San Francisco votes 'No' on Women".

8. Another possibility, not pursued by the Board but mentioned in conversation by several members, was dissolution of the Club and distribution of its assets among the members as provided by Article II, s.9 of the by-laws.

9. This has since been done.

10. The Committee's argument was one which had been heard before: that a vote ought to be held as part of a meeting.

11. But once the Supreme Court of the United States had spoken, continuing the legal battle would also have had great costs. The Olympic Club, which continued to resist demands by the city attorney of San Francisco that it accept female members, is reliably reported to have spent at least $750,000 on legal fees as of early 1990.

12. Whatever the image, the reality was better than "beef and booze"; the Club's kitchen has always maintained wide and sophisticated offerings.

CHAPTER 12

Club Life

Above all, the University Club has been a place of friendship, within which members have created their own particular circles as well as participating in the wider Club community. This creation of clubs within the Club has been a phenomenon from the earliest days, and is arguably one of the chief benefits of membership. Duck-hunters, golfers, flyfishers, trap- and skeet-shooters, wine connoisseurs and members with all sorts of other different tastes find each other in the Club. Most recently, a "wine club" has been organized within the Club on the initiative of the Wine Committee.

Perhaps its most persistent inner circle is the lunchtime "round table" in the fourth-floor bar. There, every day, an assorted collection of members take lunch. The size of this gathering varies: if it is large, the round table is extended by pushing other tables together - losing its roundness but gaining in conviviality. There, lunch is accompanied by the rattle of dice cups as members "shake" to see who will sign for a round of drinks.[1]

Predominant among the multitude of tastes to which the Club caters are those of eating, drinking and conversation, preferably in combination. Opportunities for these activities are provided in abundance. The Club year is punctuated by occasions designed to encourage them; lunches and dinners with speeches or music; events celebrating occasions

— spring and fall being the special prerogative of the oenophiles, with mother's day, Thanksgiving and Christmas also providing the opportunity to imbibe, ingest and discourse.

Special mention should be made of the annual Boxing Day luncheon, which enjoys an anomalous status, because over the years it has been organized on private initiative and therefore is not an official function. Nevertheless, it is something of a Club institution. Its stated purpose is to provide psychological relief from the horrors of the festive season, such as "the chores of shopping and being nice to all our friends, relatives, families, et cetera." With this in mind, at 1 pm on the day after Christmas a set lunch is served to those invited, the time of adjournment being left to each individual invitee; Boxing Day lunch is, for many members, a protracted affair.

The Staff

As a full-service institution, the Club could not have continued without a succession of excellent employees. Those who have been appreciated most have been the bartenders, especially those on the fourth floor. "We've always prided ourselves on our fourth floor bartenders", noted past-President Frederick O. Johnson. Glories become more glorious when recounted in the fourth floor bar, jokes a little

University Club

Dear

      I have the pleasure of informing you that you have been elected a member of the University Club

      The rules of the Club provide that a newly elected member shall sign the

By Laws and pay the Admission Fee and first month's dues within fifteen days from the notice of election

      I therefore beg to enclose herewith a bill for the initiation fee and first month's dues and to inform you that the book of By Laws will be found at the office of the Club

      Very truly yours

_ _ _ _ _ _ _ _ _ _ _ _ _ _ _ _ _ _

Secretary

_ _ _ _ _ _ _ _ 19_ _ _

San Francisco, Cal.

LEFT: *The official admission letter, sent to every prospective new member, includes a reminder to pay the initiation fee.*

funnier, and drinks taste better. Indeed, Johnson asserts that martinis are better mixed on the fourth floor than the third. Perhaps its higher altitude makes a difference.

Several bartenders, like many of the Club's employees, have been recruited from nearby Chinatown. A prototypical bartender was Hong, who started with the Club in about 1910 and remained until the 1950s. He knew everyone's name and did all his accounting on an abacus. He was remembered fondly by Chauncey McKeever: "he would stay up all night long, as long as anybody was in the Club". When Hong retired, McKeever commissioned Moya de Pino to paint his portrait, which still hangs in the clubhouse. When Hong died in January, 1967, the Club lent this portrait to be paraded at his traditional Chinese funeral.

Hong's successors have also been commemorated by paintings, including Tom, who took over from Hong in the 1950s and retired in 1977: Jerry Gouch painted his portrait. Tom's place was taken over in turn by George Jang, who had already worked for the Club for twenty years before becoming bartender. When he retired in 1987, Chauncey McKeever commissioned Suzanne Siminger to capture him on canvas.

Another servant of whom the Club retains a portrait was Lung Sung Wong, who worked in the dining room and was, according to Henry Hardy's recollection "a real leader" among its staff. In his spare time, he was a highly skilled calligrapher who for a while edited a Chinatown newspaper. On his retirement in 1981, the Board appropriated $1,200 for his portrait to be painted.

Workers in other parts of the clubhouse were also valued. Cyrilla N. Bloss, who worked in the Club's office from 1954 until June of 1978 was a great favorite, whom members saw at the front desk when they came to the Club. "To meet and greet so many nice gentlemen when they arrived for lunch was a break for me from my office duties," she reminisced. "After lunch...everything

was quiet and back to work. To me it seemed that I was hostess at a daily reception for my friends". The members apparently also felt that way; when she retired, they raised $12,000 for her as a gift and a special round table luncheon was held which Churchill Peters judged to be "the largest gathering we ever had". She wrote thanking the Club for the occasion: "I was happily surprised to realize how deeply all of you felt towards me. I shall always remember you".

During or after their service at the Club, some of the employees have prospered mightily. One, at least, has become a San Francisco landlord. An ex-waiter is a professional photographer who got his start taking pictures of the inside of the Club for insurance purposes. But most conspicuously, several of the Club's chefs have gone on to enjoy major commercial success.

The Members

Ultimately, however, the atmosphere of the Club has always depended on its members, who craft the Club's character.

Over the years, many of the west's most distinguished men have enjoyed the privilege of membership. John Muir, the conservationist; M.M. O'Shaunghessy, the engineer responsible for the Hetchy Hetchy water project and San Francisco's International Airport; William B. Bourn, owner of San Francisco's water supply; the Tobins, who controlled the Hibernia Bank; the Crockers who did likewise with the Crocker Bank; Peter Folger, the coffee king; David Star Jordan, the first president of Stanford University; Benjamin Ide Wheeler, one of the most accomplished presidents of the University of California; Luther Burbank, the outstanding botanist; William Keith, the leading landscape painter; James D. Phelan, United States Senator; and Herbert Hoover, President of the United States.

To each of these men, no doubt, the Club has had a personal significance: as an institution it has been many things to many different members. Some, through Club acquaintanceships, have vicariously shared in adventures - as when in 1906 a cross-country drive began with a bet made in the Club,[2] or when, eighty years later, Maxie Anderson planned his cross-country balloon crossing from the Club.[3] Others credit the Club as a forum for new ideas, with a part in the computer revolution.[4] But typically, the Club has offered more prosaic advantages.

For some, it has been a home, even a way of life. For easterners, still a prominent element in the Club, it has been a reminder of home. As Robert Morris put it:

> For a lot of us from the East Coast there's some things we miss...to me it's kind of an extension of being at home and what I left back in Philadelphia.

Chauncey McKeever had a different explanation for the hold the Club has on members' affections:

> When you ask what the Club is for, it's to get to know people, of being among familiar things and familiar people, familiar food. That's about

it. Coziness. Shabby-gentility, leather chairs: a good rail on the bar.

Comfort, familiarity, good company and friendship come up time and again. These have been the hallmark of the Club down the years.

One *vignette* illustrates these values. In 1969, a longtime and beloved member, Clay Miller, turned 90 years old. The members organized a special luncheon in his honor. On that occasion, Miller read one of his own poems, entitled "Counting", which he modestly described as "not very good poetry, but a good idea":

> Count your garden by the flowers
> Never by the leaves that fall.
> Count your day-to-day golden hours,
> Never mind the clouds at all.
> Count your nights by stars, not shadows;
> Count your life by faith, not fears.
> And then, with joy on every birthday,
> Count your age by friends, not years.

Notes

1. Those who want a more sedate lunch can eat at the Club table in the third floor dining room, where any member can sit and join other members who happen to be there without prior introduction.

2. In 1903, rising to the challenge of a $50 bet made in the Club, Dr Nelson Jackson began his celebrated 63 day cross-country drive in a Winton motor carriage. Thus, by making a wager, some unknown member unwittingly furthered America's love affair with the automobile.

3. Member Maxie Anderson planned his 100 hour nonstop balloon trip across North America in the Club: members Frank King and John Stuppin helped him find the lift-off site at Fort Baker in Marin County. On his return, on September 24, a special dinner in his honor was held at the Club at which he told of his adventure.

4. In 1966, discussion of computer chips with frequent Club guest Howard Bubb resulted in the building of a factory in an apricot orchard in Cupertino and a company called American Microsystems was founded, whose stock rose from $1 to $68 during the next two years: the computer revolution was on.

A Note on Sources

I t is impossible to tell every story about an institution whose length of life has reached 100 years, but in creating this narrative of the University Club of San Francisco, its writer has had many valuable sources to look at, allowing him to create a fairly complete account.

University Club Publications

Nathaniel Blaisdell's short *History*, originally published 1932 and updated by Lewis P. Mansfield in 1954, has been a major source.

Thomas Hamilton Breeze's *Round Table Sonnets* (1934) — his poetic salute to some of his best University Club friends — gave a good insight into the social atmosphere of the Club during the 1930s and is listed here although strictly it is not a Club publication, since it declares itself a product of the Grabhorn Press.

Frank T. Adams, *Songs of the University Club* (1947) illuminated the 1920s, 1930s and 1940s.

Archival and Documentary Sources

Of tremendous value to the creation of this narrative has been the University Club's oral history archive in the Bancroft Library of the University of California at Berkeley. This project was initiated in anticipation of the Club's centennial celebration. Among the recordings and transcripts deposited there and made available for the preparation of this work are the collective memories of Tindall Cashion, Leon de Fremery, Theodore L. Eliot, Henry Gifford Hardy, Frederick O. Johnson, John Lewis, Chauncey McKeever, Robert Morris, Charles Noble, Churchill C. Peters, Ignazio J. Ruvolo, I.F. Barreda Sherman, Murray Smith and William O. Sumner.

The Club's annual reports from the 1940s have been a primary source.

The Minutes of the Board of Directors have been of tremendous importance, chronicling as they do the Club's activities on a monthly and, during some difficult periods, a weekly or even daily basis. They illuminate aspects of the Club's life never before disclosed in narrative form. They also leave unanswerable historical riddles. For example, the Minutes of September 24, 1901 record without explanation, there being no allusions to the matter before or after: "It was the sense of the Board that the bills of Curtain's Detective Agency be paid". And on January 21, 1902: "The matter of an assault upon the chef by one of the waiters was left to Mr Pillsbury". Such curious references are found even in more recent times. On July 20, 1976 it was written: "a letter was read from Mr. Byron W. Leydecker apologizing for use of an old custom which caused some damage to the Directors' Room". And on May

18, 1983: "Director Robinson emphatically denounced any insinuations that he would donate the other (#+c(&c") flagpole".

Nathaniel Blaisdell, writing in 1932, thought that the fire and earthquake of 1906 had "destroyed all of the Club's records", believing that "all that was saved were the account books and the Keith picture". It is true that the Minutes from 1890-1900 were lost, but those of 1900-1906 survive. Perhaps Blaisdell categorized the surviving early Minutes along with the account books.

The only other gap in the Club's Minutes is for the ten year period 1942-1952, the loss of which can be somewhat compensated for by consultation of the annual reports.

The personal papers of two members have graciously been made available to the writer. Those of Churchill C. Peters render considerable help with the 1940s, and the late Henry Gifford Hardy's boxes of materials give much background on the entire span of the Club's existence. Hardy had gathered letters, papers, and news clippings and written up various episodes in the life of the Club with the intention of compiling its history himself.

Additionally, the unpublished memoirs of Leon de Fremery, who was president during the Club's most perilous period (1944-47) have been used.

Informal Sources

The writer has had conversations and interviews with various members. In addition, information provided by the Club's current manager, Desmond Elder, has been helpful as has that from the Club's squash professional, John Lau.

General San Francisco and California Sources

Many California and San Francisco historical publications dating from the turn of the century have been consulted. In addition, newspapers, San Francisco City Directories, the social *Blue Books* for various years and the files of the San Francisco Public Library History Room have been drawn upon.

Comparative Sources

Some references to the centennial histories of two sister clubs of approximately the University Club's age have been given for comparative purposes. They are:

Timothy F. Comstock, *The Sutter Club — One Hundred Years* (Sacramento: The Sutter Club, 1989), cited throughout as Comstock 1989, and

Reginald H. Roy, *The Vancouver Club — First Century, 1889-1989* (Vancouver, B.C.: The Vancouver Club, 1989), cited as Roy 1989.

Picture Sources

All illustrations in this book are from Club archives unless otherwise listed below as having another source. In all such cases, the illustrations are reproduced with permission.

1. The picture of the Club's site when it was still occupied by Leland Stanford's stables comes from the History Department of Wells Fargo Bank, and is panel no. 5 of the San Francisco panorama photographed by Eadweard Muybridge in 1877.

2. The Library of Congress supplied the following pictures:

a. the palazzo Medici (now Riccardi), Florence, Italy; and

b. the panoramic view of San Francisco, looking towards Nob Hill, directly after the 1906 earthquake.

3. The following illustrations come from the History Room of the San Francisco Public Library:

a. the picture of William Thomas, reproduced from *San Francisco: Its Builders Past and Present* (1913);

b. the picture of Willis Polk's design for a

clubhouse at the corner of Van Ness Avenue and Sutter Street, reproduced from the architect's original prospectus;

c. the doctored photograph of Fairmont Hotel being used as a heliport.

4. The Club bill to the Rev. A. Crosby, dated December 7, 1897, is reproduced by the permission of a member.

5. The Club is indebted to Daisy G. Yee for the following color pictures, taken especially for this book:

a. the stained glass of the coat of arms of the University of Santiago, Chile;

b. the view from the Club balcony towards the San Francisco Residence Club;

c. the exterior of the present clubhouse; and

d. Hermes in his garden.

The Clubhouse
by Kevin Tierney

The University Club of San Francisco has been in uninterrupted possession of its own purpose-built clubhouse at 800 Powell Street, on the northeastern corner of California and Powell, since October 1909. Initially, the Club was a tenant of the trustees of the Leland Stanford Jr. University under a thirty-year lease; then (from February, 1929) the trustees' mortgagor; and finally, in May of 1962, it became an absolute owner.

The Architects

The Stanford trustees required the Club to construct a class C building at a cost of between $100,000 and $150,000 but otherwise gave the Club a free hand, including the right to pick the architects. The Club's choice fell upon Walter Bliss and William Faville, both graduates of the Massachusetts Institute of Technology who had worked in the offices of the famous New York architectural firm of McKim, Mead & White before moving to San Francisco in the early 1890s.[1] There, they learned to combine modern engineering techniques with classical forms.

It is not known why the Club retained Bliss & Faville rather than going back to Willis Polk, who had won the Club's architectural competition in 1904 with a design for a clubhouse to be put up at the corner of Sutter Street and Van Ness Avenue.[2] Possibly, there was ill-feeling between Polk and the

Club because the Club had not used Polk's 1904 plans, but it is more likely that after the earthquake he had enough work and was known not to be available for further commissions.

Even before the 1906 earthquake, Bliss & Faville enjoyed a substantial practice; their most important pre-earthquake building was the St. Francis Hotel (1904).[3] The partnership's prestige was enhanced by the fact that the hotel's walls remained standing after the earthquake (although its interior was completely gutted by fire); this may have influenced their retention by the Club. Anyway, their choice ensured a clubhouse of traditional rather than *avant garde* appearance.[4]

The Site

The clubhouse site, a good but not commanding position on the eastern slope of Nob Hill, had previously been occupied by Leland Stanford's stables; his mansion had been diagonally opposite on the southwestern corner of California and Powell Streets.

Bliss & Faville showed particular skill in responding to the unusual challenge presented by the site, which is on northward and easterly gradients.[5] The steepness of the slope down California Street to the financial district required that a rectangular excavation be made into the side of the hill and made it expedient that the Club's front entrance would face

Powell rather than California Street, even though its slope meant that the back of the building would be exceptionally exposed.

The site's immediate surroundings were also demanding. From the start, the architects had to take into account the massive presence of the Fairmont Hotel which, having survived the earthquake, would overshadow the new clubhouse. Furthermore, directly to the south on California Street, the Alta Casa apartment building was about to go up[6] and it was inevitable that the site of the Stanford mansion would be redeveloped soon. Thus, if the clubhouse was to stand out, it would not do so because of height or size. The solution adopted was to distinguish the building by a design in a style not otherwise represented on Nob Hill and by use of a facing of terracota brickwork instead of stone.[7] This was an innovation, but not incongruous; indeed, it anticipated the rustication of many later classically modeled buildings.

The Exterior

The clubhouse owes nothing to either of San Francisco's indigenous "mission" or "gingerbread" styles, the flamboyance of which it eschews. Still less does it ape Chicago's skyscrapers or the more recumbent modernism of Frank Lloyd Wright. Rather, its exterior is renaissance-derived Italianate, the renaissance style probably being regarded as suitable for a "university" club because it evoked the ideal of the renaissance man to which higher education paid lip service.

The clubhouse is based upon the palazzo Medici (subsequently known as Riccardi) in Florence and the palazzo Farnese in Rome,[8] the former's influence being predominant. Its *facade* is of four horizontal stories (one more than either of its antecedents), the two uppers being loftier than the lowers. It is precise and restrained, although not devoid of decoration, having, for instance, an unemblazoned oval shield

with two side supporters above its central doorway - a simplified version of a popular Italian conceit.[9] From the front the building has a satisfying symmetry, with a surprising lightness in view of its mass. A consequence of its apparent completeness is that it has defied extension or expansion; when the Club has built (and it has rebuilt its squash courts twice),[10] it has put up entirely separate structures.[11]

The Interior

The unity of the outside of the Club disguises its considerable interior diversity.

By contrast with its Italianate exterior, the inspiration of the clubhouse interior is that of an English country house. Unlike the architects of some other clubs elsewhere, Bliss & Faville did not try to evoke an idealized generic campus. Chicago's University Club, for instance, has rooms with names like "college hall" and "cathedral room", presenting versions of a college refectory that are actually far grander than anything the colleges attended by most of its members can boast. But 800 Powell is more domestic in intent, carrying forward somewhat the style set at 722 Sutter Street, the Club's previous premises.

Reflecting the professional convention of their times, Bliss & Faville did not design a mere shell; their plans incorporated a multitude of interior details.[12] However, in contrast to the exterior, the original floorplans have been extensively changed over the years and the late I.F. Barreda Sherman's recollection that the clubhouse of the early 1980s had not changed much since the 1920s is misleading. In consequence, only a few of the building's many fine internal features can be discussed with confidence that they reflect Bliss & Faville's vision, rather than later alterations. Below is an attempt to identify the surviving original configurations of each floor, followed by an epitome of the principal changes made since 1909.

Selected Surviving Original Features of the Clubhouse Interior

1. Fourth floor.
The only two fourth floor rooms which remain

largely as Bliss & Faville designed them are, respectively, its grandest and most intimate rooms - the lounge and the library.

(a) *The Lounge*: The lounge is airy and light, taking advantage of its superb east-facing view over downtown. It is decorated by low relief pilasters surmounted by Ionic capitals, the distinctive *volutes* of which add interest to the ceiling line.

Bliss & Faville knew that the Club's William Keith landscape (salvaged from 722 Sutter Street) would be placed above the lounge fireplace and this no doubt dictated its size and the happy choice of its veined burgundy-brown marble.

(b) *The Library*: The library is as intimate as a private home's, but too dark. This, however, is not Bliss & Faville's fault; they intended an additional window on its north side, which was eliminated.[13] The library's darkness has not been totally undesirable; its eastern light sometimes creates a fascinating *chiaroscuro* in late afternoon.

The library's floor-to-ceiling fitted wooden bookshelves are fine, but (1990) in need of refinishing.

2. Third floor.
The dining room, directly below the fourth floor lounge, is the only room on this floor remaining largely unchanged. Like the lounge above, its windows take advantage of its eastern view. The stained glasses of university insignia make a colorful frieze across the top of its eastern wall.

There is a handsome carved fireplace at the dining room's north end.

3. Second floor.
Unlike the top two floors, this floor was never intended for display; it has always been bedrooms.

4. First floor.
There is little of architectural note on the first floor. The front lobby is paneled.

5. Basement.
Bliss & Faville left the basement unfinished; it was

not used as recreational space until the 1950s, when it became a bar and dining room. Reconstruction was begun in the late 1980s, but suspended in 1988. The basement remained closed as of 1990.

Principal Interior Changes to the Clubhouse since 1909

The principal changes have been:

1. Fourth floor.
Circa 1916, the "periodicals room" (also known as the "writing room") on the southeastern corner (now the game room) was converted into a grill room.

The fourth floor bar was repositioned, from the northwest corner to the southwest, in 1935. Previously, the southwest corner had been a billiard room. The part of the bar nearest to the elevator was originally a card room. There was substantial renovation of the bar in 1966.

The northwest corner bar space vacated in 1935 was converted into a poolroom and then, in 1967-68, when usage had diminished, into the directors' dining room.

The fourth-floor lounge was redecorated 1951-1953.

In the early fifties, the corridor leading to the library began to be used as exhibition space for Club artists. This space was named the Henry Hardy gallery in 1972.

New carpet was installed in the library in 1959, but otherwise this room is virtually unchanged since the opening of the clubhouse.

2. Third floor.
Three original bedrooms (and their shared parlor) were eliminated, apparently in the 1930s, from the space now occupied by the third-floor bar.

In the main dining room, a stained glass commemorating the University of Santiago, Chile, was installed in 1925 and an additional seven were installed to honor other universities in 1952.

There was a partial redecoration of the main dining room in 1942 and a complete one in 1949-1951 and again in the 1980s.

The kitchen was overhauled 1947-1949, and again in 1986.

3. Second floor.
This floor has always been largely devoted to bedrooms which, however, have been substantially remodeled three times. As early as 1918, when the clubhouse was only nine years old, all the bedrooms facing east (on both the first and second floor) were widened to give each two windows and a separate bathroom, cutting down the total number of bedrooms by three or four. This reflected a change in social standards. When the clubhouse was designed, separate bathrooms were not expected; a decade later, they were. (As originally designed, both the first and second floors were provided with a "public" bathroom - i.e., one used in common by all residents who did not have bath facilities *en suite*).

The second renovation took place in 1954, but was less visible than those that preceded or succeeded it, being largely ancillary to the replacement of the old plumbing. At this time, the Cable Car room was refurbished (and was further upgraded in 1958).

The third renovation occurred in 1978, when the Club decided that it would no longer accommodate permanent residents and upgraded the bedrooms for rental to members' guests and members of other clubs with which reciprocal arrangements existed.

4. First floor.
Beginning in 1959 and continuing into the sixties, the entrance lobby was remodeled. In order to increase floor space, the original revolving door at the front entrance was replaced by the present hinged door.

The old coat and hat room was only half the size of the present one; much of the area it now occupies was a small reception room, now eliminated. A small part of that reception room was used to create the manager's office.

5. Basement.
The basement was virtually unfinished until 1957, but it is a myth that the cobbled floor of Leland Stanford's stable was still visible until then. In 1957, it was opened as a bar and a dining room was added in 1963.

Renovations authorized in 1987 were suspended indefinitely in 1989 because of cost.

An Appraisal

The only excuse for offering a brief appraisal of the Club's building here is that it has not had the critical attention it deserves; amazingly, the principal modern guide to San Francisco architecture does not so much as mention the Club.[14]

The clubhouse successfully combines a classical form with early twentieth century engineering on a difficult site. Arguably, the building's aesthetic values have stood the test of time rather better than its engineering, because its unfussy exterior anticipated later architectural tastes - but nothing should be said against its engineering, which was vindicated by the fact that the building came through the earthquake of October 1989 unscathed.

Notes

1. See Richard Longstreth, *On the Edge of the World* (New York: The Architectural History Foundation, 1983), p.297.

2. Polk had apprenticed in the Chicago office of Burnham & Root in the same way that Bliss & Faville had trained at McKim, Mead & White in New York. The Club used good architects.

3. Subsequently, Bliss & Faville enjoyed tremendous success. Apart from the University Club, their principal works in San Francisco were:
    - 400 California Street (the old Bank of America building), 1908;
    - 1 Market Street (the Southern Pacific building), 1915;
    - 2222 Broadway (the former Flood mansion, now the

Convent of the Sacred Heart), 1916;
- 640 Sutter Street (the Women's Athletic Club, now known as the Metropolitan Club), 1916-22;
- 350 McAllister Street (the State of California office building), 1922-1926.

4. None of the other successful bay area architects of the period, such as Bernard Maybeck, Julia Morgan or Willis Polk, was "modern".

5. The Club's horizontal building line, like that of many Nob Hill structures, diverges from the angle of the sidewalk.

6. Long since demolished. The site is now a parking lot.

7. The only other brick building of exterior distinction nearby was Old St. Mary's below the Club at the corner of California Street and Dupont (now Grant) Avenue.

8. Bliss & Faville may have followed fashionable Club architecture in New York and London as closely as the Italian models. The University Club of New York is also based upon the palazzo Medici (now Riccardi) in Florence and Sir Charles Barry's design for the Reform Club in London (1837) is based on Rome's palazzo Farnese.

9. Similar ornamentation survives on the contemporaneous Native Sons of the Golden West building at 414 Mason Street.

10. The first squash court was built 1929, a second was added in 1932 and a completely rebuilt facility was opened in 1976.

11. "Who could add anything to a Greek temple that would not be an obvious excrescence?" H.D.F. Kitto, *The Greeks* (1951), p.183.

12. In addition, Bliss & Faville were almost certainly consulted about the building's original furniture, the main items of which cost the Club nearly $30,000 - an amount equal to 20% of the cost of the clubhouse.

13. Bliss & Faville's sketch of the front elevation of the clubhouse in their prospectus of 1908 shows 830 Powell Street's site as vacant.

14. David Gebhard, Eric Sandweiss and Robert Winter, eds., *Architecture in San Francisco and Northern California* (Salt Lake City: Gibbs M. Smith, Inc., 1985).

THE EXPOSITI

SAN FRAN